D0546193

PASTA
SAUCES

FRANCES CLEARY

CONTENTS

The Author   3

Introduction   4

Traditional Sauces   11

Meat and Fish Sauces   31

Vegetarian Sauces   51

Baked Pasta Dishes   81

Index to Recipes   95

Published exclusively for J Sainsbury plc
Stamford House Stamford Street
London SE1 9LL
by Martin Books
Simon & Schuster Consumer Group
Grafton House 64 Maids Causeway
Cambridge CB5 8DD

First published April 1992
Second impression July 1992

ISBN 0 85941 765 4

Text, photographs and illustrations
© 1992, J Sainsbury plc

Printed in Italy by Printer Trento

THE AUTHOR

Frances Cleary grew up in New England in the United States. She read modern languages at university and developed a passion for French and Italian cookery while travelling abroad as a student. Subsequently she earned the Grand Diplôme in Cuisine and Pâtisserie from the Cordon Bleu Cookery School in Paris.

Frances now lives in London, where she specialises in cookery writing, recipe development and food styling. She also gives demonstrations and private cookery lessons.

INTRODUCTION

Pasta is the cornerstone of the Italian diet, as important to daily living as bread to the French or rice to the Chinese. Most Italians eat pasta every day, consuming 24 kg (55 lb) per person annually, compared with only 2.75 kg (6 lb) per person in Great Britain. This difference is even more remarkable when you consider that, for us, pasta typically constitutes the

Puttanesca Sauce (page 29)

Pesto (Basil sauce, page 18)

main course of a meal, while for the Italians it is usually only served as a starter.

How do the Italians manage to eat so much pasta without becoming bored with it? The answer, of course, lies in the huge variety of sauces they serve with it. Whether meat-, fish- or vegetable-based, there are literally hundreds of sauces for pasta, both traditional and new.

In fact, there are at least 30 variations of that old standby, basic tomato sauce, known as Pommarola (Neapolitan tomato sauce, page 12)

picy Ground Turkey auce (page 35)

in Italy. Amatrice Sauce (page 16) is basic
tomato sauce which has bacon and crushed
chillies added to it. Puttanesca Sauce (page 29)
is a tomato sauce made with anchovies, black
olives and capers. There are endless other
variations. Contrary to popular opinion,
however, the well-known Ragù alla
Bolognese (Bolognese sauce, page 23) is not
made with tomatoes. Instead, it owes its
characteristic rich flavour to a long, slow
cooking process.

Pasta-based meals are the ideal way for
every busy working person to get a nutritious
meal on the table at the end of a long day. With
a few basic cupboard ingredients, such as
canned tomatoes, canned tuna, canned
anchovies or jars of olives, a delicious meal can
be prepared quickly and easily. Most varieties
of pasta take less than 15 minutes to cook and
the majority of the pasta sauces in this book
take less than 30 minutes to prepare.

Do not overlook pasta's health benefits
either. Pasta is low in fat and high in
carbohydrate, so when combined with a low-
fat sauce it is the ideal way to reduce fat
consumption in line with current dietary
guidelines. Vegetable sauces such as Pasta
Primavera (page 60) and pulse-based sauces are
a delicious and healthy alternative to meat-
based sauces, and inexpensive to make as well!

PASTA VARIETIES
The basic ingredients of dried pasta, the kind
we buy in packets at the supermarket, are flour
and water. Different coloured pasta can be
obtained by adding tomato, egg or spinach (as
in red, white and green fusilli tricolori, which
represents the colours of the Italian flag).
Durum wheat is the name of the flour used to
make most pasta. It is a coarse flour consisting
of the durum flour and the hard grains of
wheat left after milling. Originally, pasta
shapes such as tagliatelle and lasagne were
made by rolling the dough out by hand and
then cutting it into the appropriate shape. The

Preparation and cooking times
Preparation and cooking times are included at the head of the recipes as a general guide; preparation times, especially, are approximate and timings are usually rounded to the nearest 5 minutes.

Preparation times include the time taken to prepare ingredients in the list, but not to make any 'basic' recipe.

The cooking times given at the heads of the recipes denote cooking periods when the dish can be left largely unattended, e.g. baking, stewing, and not the total amount of cooking for the recipe. Always read and follow the timings given for the steps of the recipe in the method.

pasta was then dried out of doors. Today pasta is made in many places besides Italy, as the drying process is controlled by modern methods. Dried pasta has a long shelf life and can be stored for 18 months to 2 years before the packet is opened.

Fresh pasta is also made with durum wheat, but eggs are used instead of or as well as water to give it a softer texture. Fresh pasta is more expensive than dried, and you will need double the dried weight to obtain the same amount of cooked pasta. It will usually keep for a few days in the refrigerator – check the 'use by' date on the packet – or it can be frozen.

Fortunately a good selection of pasta shapes is available in Britain. Sainsbury's stocks many different types and shapes of both dried and fresh pasta.

COOKING AND SERVING PASTA-BASED DISHES
Not surprisingly, there is a loose set of rules governing which type of sauce should accompany which variety of pasta. The texture, thickness and shape of the pasta play a role in determining this pairing. Generally speaking, long pasta such as capellini or fettuccine goes best with tomato- or fish-based sauces, whereas heavier cream- or meat-based sauces are better with shorter shapes such as macaroni or penne. The texture and hollowness of the shorter shapes mean that they can soak up thicker sauces, making them an ideal partner. It is worth bearing in mind that these are only rough guidelines, however, as the combination of spaghetti and bolognese sauce is a favourite the world over, even though it doesn't fit neatly into either of these categories! Each recipe in this book gives suggestions for the best type of pasta to serve with the sauce, but the choice really depends on personal preference. Do not hesitate to mix and match pasta shapes and sauces, and if you prefer one particular shape to another, use it whenever you wish.

A PASTA GLOSSARY

Choosing the right sauce is still only half the story, however, as there is also a set of simple rules concerning the proper way to cook pasta. To begin with, many of the sauces in this book will cook in the same amount of time or just a little longer than the time it takes for the pasta to cook, so in these cases the best rule is to put the pasta water on to boil as soon as, or not

CANNELLONI *Large, hollow tubes which are usually stuffed with meat, vegetables or fish, covered with a sauce and then baked.*

CAPELLINI *A very fine version of spaghetti, also known as 'angel hair'. It is excellent for a light meal. Its chief virtue lies in its quick cooking time of 2–3 minutes.*

CONCHIGLIE *In the shape of a shell, this smooth or ridged pasta looks lovely with seafood sauces.*

FUSILLI *A spiral- or corkscrew-shaped pasta, which works well with all sauces. Wholewheat spirals are also available.*

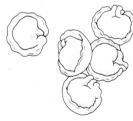

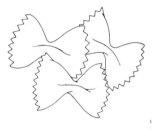

CAPPELLETTI *Stuffed pasta resembling small hats, which its name means in Italian. It is a versatile shape which can be used in soups or served with sauces.*

FARFALLE *Commonly known as 'bows', the name actually means 'butterflies' in Italian. It is best suited to light sauces.*

LASAGNE *Large, rectangular sheets which are used in baked dishes. Lasagne are available in green and white and wholewheat.*

LINGUINE *A thin, ribbon-shaped pasta. Its name means 'little tongues'.*

FETTUCCINE *A ribbon-shaped pasta, available in green and white. Fettuccine are excellent with most pasta sauces.*

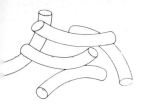

MACARONI *Small, hollow tubes which are often called 'elbows' because of their curved shape. Good in baked dishes or with sauces.*

long after, you start cooking the sauce. Use a large, tall pan which can hold plenty of water and add salt to taste if wished as soon as the water is boiling rapidly. Add the pasta all at once and give it a quick stir to prevent sticking. It is impossible to give exact times for cooking dried pasta, as different brands vary. Check the packet instructions and test a small

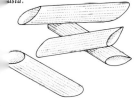

PAGLIA E FIENO *A pasta whose name means 'straw and hay'. Paglia e Fieno are long, narrow ribbons of green and white pasta.*

RAVIOLI *A square-shaped pasta which usually has a scalloped edge. Ravioli generally have a meat or cheese stuffing and are best with light cream- or tomato-based sauces.*

TAGLIATELLE *Flat ribbon noodles which are slightly wider than fettuccine. Available in green and white, tagliatelle go well with most sauces.*

PENNE *A ribbed or smooth, short, tubular pasta with ends cut at an angle to resemble a quill, the translation of its Italian name. Penne go best with thick meat sauces.*

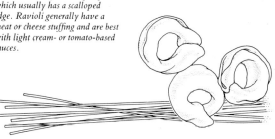

SPAGHETTI *Spaghetti is the most popular and best known pasta shape worldwide. It consists of long, thin strands and can be served with virtually any sauce.*

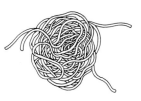

TORTELLONI *A stuffed pasta shape, filled with either a meat, cheese or spinach and ricotta stuffing. Tortelloni should be served with light, simple sauces.*

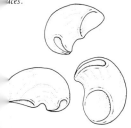

PIPE RIGATE *A shell-shaped pasta, similar to conchiglie, with a ribbed surface. A perfect partner for thick sauces.*

TAGLIARINI *A long, thin, ribbon-shaped pasta usually sold in a nest shape. They are available in a pretty combination of red, white and green, the colours of the Italian flag.*

VERMICELLI *A very thin version of spaghetti, it comes shaped in a nest which uncoils whilst cooking. Vermicelli are often used in soups or served with delicate sauces.*

9

piece of pasta every now and then as it cooks. It should be *al dente* – firm to the bite. Overcooked or undercooked pasta will ruin a dish, so drain it at exactly the right moment. The Italians do not shake off all the water clinging to the pasta, as this interferes with the absorption of the sauce. Never leave pasta sitting in the colander without tossing it with some oil or butter or it will stick together. When cooking fresh pasta the same method is followed, although the cooking time is considerably shorter, usually 3–4 minutes.

When serving pasta, the Italians prefer to serve long pasta, such as spaghetti, tagliatelle and capellini, on individual plates with the sauce on top to be mixed in at the table. Pasta shapes, such as pipe rigate, farfalle and conchiglie, are generally mixed with the sauce in a large bowl before reaching the table, so that the sauce can get into all the crevices. These are not hard and fast rules, however, and as with the pairing of pasta shapes and sauces, the choice is really yours.

It is difficult to recommend the amount of pasta to cook as so much depends on personal appetite. As a guideline, allow 75–100 g (3–4 oz) of dried pasta per adult for a main meal and 50–75 g (2–3 oz) for a starter or small helping. You will need double the quantity if using fresh pasta. Most of the sauces in this book are intended for 4 people as a main course or for 6 people as a starter. If you find that appetites in your household require more or less pasta, adjust the quantity to suit your needs.

My final recommendation for preparing the recipes in this book is not to skimp on good quality ingredients. When making tomato sauces with fresh tomatoes, use ripe plum tomatoes as they give the best flavour. Use fresh herbs if possible, especially fresh basil, and try to buy fresh parmesan cheese to grate yourself. Above all, treat yourself and your family to a lovely bottle of extra-virgin olive oil. Your efforts will be rewarded.

TRADITIONAL SAUCES

SUGO DI NOCI

Walnut sauce   Serves 4

Preparation time: 10 minutes

175 g (6 oz) walnut pieces

75–125 g (3–4 oz) parsley, preferably flat-leaf, chopped finely

4 tablespoons fresh breadcrumbs

100 g (3½ oz) butter, softened

125 ml (4 fl oz) olive oil

4 tablespoons double cream

salt and pepper

parsley sprigs, to garnish

Walnut sauce is a speciality of Liguria, a region known for its temperate climate. Walnut trees grow abundantly in Southern Italy, but recipes using walnuts are more common in the north. Try this one with tagliatelle verdi.

Preheat the oven to Gas Mark 4/180°C/350°F or preheat the grill. Toast 50 g (2 oz) of the walnuts for 3–5 minutes. Reserve for the garnish.

Place the remaining walnuts, the parsley and the breadcrumbs in a food processor or blender and chop until finely ground. Add the butter and oil and blend again to form a thick green paste. Blend in the cream and adjust the seasoning.

Pour the sauce over freshly cooked pasta and toss well. Garnish with the reserved walnuts and parsley sprigs.

POMMAROLA

Neapolitan tomato sauce   Serves 4

Preparation time: 5 minutes + 25–30 minutes cooking

4 tablespoons olive oil

2 garlic cloves, chopped

500 g (1 lb) ripe tomatoes, skinned and chopped coarsely, or a 397 g (14 oz) can of chopped tomatoes

1 tablespoon finely chopped fresh oregano

1 teaspoon sugar

salt and pepper

oregano sprigs, to garnish

This classic tomato sauce originated in the sunny south-western seaport of Naples. It is best made with fresh, ripe tomatoes, but canned may be used. Serve with tortelloni or ravioli.

Heat the oil in a saucepan and gently fry the garlic for 2 minutes. Add the remaining ingredients and cook over a moderately high heat for 25–30 minutes, uncovered, until thickened, stirring frequently. Serve with freshly cooked pasta, garnished with fresh oregano sprigs.

Spinach and Ricotta Sauce

Sugo di Noci (Walnut sauce)

Pommarola (Neapolitan tomato sauce)

SPINACH AND RICOTTA SAUCE

Serves 4

Preparation time: 15 minutes + about 10 minutes cooking

1 kg (2 lb) fresh spinach, stalks removed, or 500 g (1 lb) frozen spinach, thawed and chopped

125 g (4 oz) butter

2 shallots, chopped finely

a pinch of freshly grated nutmeg

125 g (4 oz) ricotta cheese, crumbled

50 g (2 oz) parmesan cheese, grated finely

salt and pepper

This is delicious served with a mixture of tagliatelle verdi and egg tagliatelle.

Place the fresh spinach in a large saucepan. Cook in 1 cm (½ inch) of boiling salted water for 5 minutes. Drain, squeezing out as much water as possible, and then chop finely. If you are using frozen spinach, squeeze out as much water as possible with your hands.

In a frying pan, melt 25 g (1 oz) of the butter. Add the shallots and fry gently for about 5 minutes until softened. Add the spinach and nutmeg and season well. Cook for 2 minutes longer and then remove from the heat.

Toss the remaining butter, the spinach mixture and the cheeses with freshly cooked pasta and mix thoroughly. Adjust the seasoning.

SEAFOOD SAUCE

Serves 4

Preparation time: 15–30 minutes + 10 minutes cooking

750 g (1½ lb) fresh mussels

750 g (1½ lb) fresh baby clams, or a 290 g (10 oz) can of baby clams in brine, drained

4 tablespoons olive oil

1 garlic clove, halved

10 spring onions, sliced diagonally into 1 cm (½-inch) pieces

4 tablespoons white wine

This black, white and green sauce looks exceptionally pretty on black squid ink pasta. This pasta can be bought in delicatessens and wholefoods shops. It looks absolutely stunning and is ideal for entertaining. Tagliatelle and fettuccine are good alternatives.

Discard any mussels that are open and do not close when tapped sharply on the work surface. Scrub the closed mussels under cold running water and remove the beards.

If using fresh clams, thoroughly scrub them with a stiff brush and soak in a sink full of cold water for 5 minutes. Drain and repeat the

2 tablespoons chopped fresh parsley, preferably flat-leaf

salt and pepper

scrubbing and soaking procedures twice more.

Combine the clams, if fresh, with the mussels in a large heavy saucepan, cover and cook (without liquid) over a high heat for 5 minutes, shaking the pan occasionally, until the shells open. Discard any that do not open. Drain them through muslin, reserving the cooking liquid. Remove most of the clams and mussels from their shells, reserving some in their shells to garnish.

In a frying pan heat the olive oil and fry the garlic and spring onions for 5 minutes, stirring. Remove and discard the garlic halves. Add the wine and 150 ml (¼ pint) of the reserved cooking liquid and reduce for 2 minutes. Add the shelled mussels and shelled or canned clams and remove the pan from the heat.

Stir in the chopped parsley and seasoning. Toss with freshly cooked pasta and garnish with the reserved clams (if using fresh) and mussels in their shells.

BAKED TOMATO SAUCE

Serves 4–6

Preparation time: 10 minutes + 30 minutes cooking

2 × 397 g (14 oz) can of chopped tomatoes

2 garlic cloves, crushed

1 onion, chopped finely

125 ml (4 fl oz) olive oil

¼ teaspoon dried crushed chillies

40 g (1½ oz) fresh breadcrumbs

40 g (1½ oz) parmesan cheese, grated

1 tablespoon shredded fresh basil

fresh basil leaves, to garnish

Strictly speaking, this is not a traditional tomato sauce, although it bears a strong resemblance to one. I have included it here because it answers every working person's prayer for a quick meal to put on the table. Try it with tortelloni or cappelletti.

Preheat the oven to Gas Mark 6/200°C/400°F. Combine the tomatoes, garlic, onion, olive oil and crushed chillies in an ovenproof dish.

Mix the breadcrumbs and parmesan cheese together and sprinkle over the tomato mixture. Bake in the oven, uncovered, for 30 minutes.

Mix the sauce into freshly cooked pasta, with the shredded basil. Garnish with fresh basil leaves.

CARBONARA SAUCE

Serves 4

Preparation time: 10 minutes + 10 minutes cooking

175 g (6 oz) smoked streaky bacon, chopped

2 tablespoons sunflower oil

250 g (8 oz) mushrooms, sliced

3 egg yolks, beaten

142 ml (¼ pint) carton of single cream

4 tablespoons chopped fresh parsley

¼ teaspoon grated nutmeg

salt and pepper

To garnish and serve:

chopped fresh parsley

freshly grated parmesan cheese

This traditional sauce is named after the Italian charcoal makers, who often made it; it was then made popular by the Allied Forces after the Second World War.

Don't worry about the eggs not being cooked in this sauce: tossing them with the hot pasta – usually spaghetti – cooks them.

Fry the bacon in the oil until crisp. Remove the bacon from the pan. Drain all but 1 tablespoon of the fat from the pan. Fry the mushrooms for about 4 minutes until soft.

Add the egg yolks and cream to freshly cooked pasta and toss well. Mix in the bacon, mushrooms, parsley, nutmeg and seasoning. Garnish with parsley and serve with parmesan cheese.

AMATRICE SAUCE

Serves 4

Preparation time: 5 minutes + 25–30 minutes cooking

175 g (6 oz) streaky bacon, cubed

2 tablespoons olive oil

1 small onion, chopped

¼ teaspoon dried crushed chillies

397 g (14 oz) can of chopped tomatoes

75 g (3 oz) parmesan cheese, grated finely

salt and pepper

This is my favourite pasta sauce. Its beauty lies in the fact that you are likely to have all the ingredients to hand. It is traditionally eaten with bucatini pasta, a very thick spaghetti strand; however, fettuccine or tagliatelle will do very well.

Fry the bacon in the olive oil for 10 minutes. Remove the bacon from the pan with a slotted spoon and drain on kitchen paper.

Carbonara Sauc
Amatrice Sauc

16

Drain off all but 1 tablespoon of the oil from the pan, add the onion, crushed chillies and tomatoes and cook for 5 minutes, stirring occasionally. Return the bacon to the pan and cook for 10–15 minutes, until the sauce thickens. Adjust the seasoning.

Toss freshly cooked pasta with the sauce and stir in the parmesan cheese.

PESTO

Basil sauce (Pictured on page 4 and on back cover)   Serves 4

Preparation time: 20 minutes

50 g (2 oz) fresh basil
125 ml (4 fl oz) olive oil
25 g (1 oz) pine kernels
2 garlic cloves, crushed
a pinch of salt
65 g (2½ oz) grated parmesan cheese
3 tablespoons ricotta cheese, crumbled
25 g (1 oz) butter, softened
fresh basil leaves, to garnish

This is a classic Italian sauce which is at its best in the summer months when fresh basil is abundant. It is traditionally made with a pestle and mortar, hence its name. It is a quick sauce to make and is particularly good with capellini. Be sure to use an extra-virgin olive oil for the best flavour.

Combine the basil, olive oil, pine kernels, garlic and salt in a food processor or blender and process until well mixed.

Transfer the mixture to a mixing bowl. Stir in the parmesan and ricotta, mixing well. Add the softened butter and stir well to combine.

Serve with freshly cooked pasta and garnish with fresh basil leaves.

BACON AND ROSEMARY SAUCE

Serves 4

Preparation time: 10 minutes + 25–30 minutes cooking

50 g (2 oz) butter
300 g (10 oz) streaky bacon, chopped
2 garlic cloves, chopped
397 g (14 oz) can of chopped tomatoes, drained

Rosemary gives this sauce a lovely delicate flavour, which goes well with spaghetti.

Melt the butter in a frying pan and fry the bacon for 10 minutes, stirring frequently. Remove the bacon from the pan with a slotted spoon and drain on kitchen paper.

Drain off all but 1 tablespoon of fat from the

2 tablespoons chopped fresh rosemary or 1 tablespoon dried rosemary

pepper

pan and add the garlic and tomatoes. Cook for 5 minutes, stirring frequently. Stir the bacon and rosemary into the tomatoes and cook for 10–15 minutes, stirring frequently, until the sauce thickens. Season with pepper and serve with freshly cooked pasta.

CALAMARI SAUCE

Serves 4

Preparation time: 30 minutes + 5 minutes cooking

1 kg (2 lb) squid

125 g (4 oz) butter

4 garlic cloves, chopped finely

3 tablespoons chopped fresh parsley, preferably flat-leaf

grated zest and juice of 1 large lemon

salt and pepper

lemons slices, to garnish

The pink and white of the squid rings looks extremely attractive against tagliatelle verdi, making this a perfect dish for entertaining. Calamari (squid) is both inexpensive and often under-rated. Be sure not to cook the squid for longer than 3 minutes or it will become tough and rubbery.

To prepare the squid, pull the head, soft innards and transparent spine out of the pouch (1). Peel the reddish membrane off the body and rinse the inside to remove the mucous membrane. Cut the eyes from the rest of the head (2). Slice the body into rings and the tentacles into small pieces (3).

In a large frying pan melt the butter until bubbling and add the garlic. Fry the squid quickly for about 3 minutes, turning once.

Add the parsley and lemon zest and juice. Season with salt and pepper. Toss with freshly cooked pasta and garnish with lemon slices.

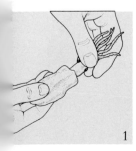

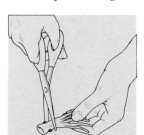

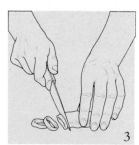

1

2

3

Crispy Parsley and
Breadcrumb Sauce

Calamari Sauce

CREAMY CHEESE SAUCE

Serves 4

Preparation time: 5 minutes

75 g (3 oz) butter

50 g (2 oz) Gruyère cheese, grated

50 g (2 oz) parmesan cheese, grated

175 ml (6 fl oz) double cream

½ teaspoon salt

pepper

fresh parsley leaves, preferably flat-leaf, to garnish

You can use fettuccine or tagliatelle for this dish. Fettuccine is the Roman version of tagliatelle and is slightly narrower and thicker.

Stir the butter, cheeses, cream and seasoning into freshly cooked pasta. Return the pasta to the pan it was cooked in. Toss lightly with two forks to mix. Serve immediately in a warmed serving bowl, garnished with parsley.

Creamy Cheese Sauce

CRISPY PARSLEY AND BREADCRUMB SAUCE

Serves 4

Preparation time: 15 minutes + 15 minutes cooking

125 ml (4 fl oz) olive oil	
3 garlic cloves, chopped finely	
50 g (2 oz) finely chopped fresh parsley, preferably flat-leaf	
1 dried red chilli, crushed	
25 g (1 oz) butter	
50 g (2 oz) fresh breadcrumbs	
fresh parsley leaves, to garnish	

I adore the flavour of crispy fried parsley. For a change, try substituting whichever fresh herbs you have to hand; fried sage is particularly nice. For a more nutty flavour, try using wholemeal breadcrumbs. This sauce is best served with vermicelli.

Heat all but 2 tablespoons of the oil in a large, shallow frying pan over a medium heat. Add the garlic, parsley and chilli and fry for 2 minutes, stirring constantly.

Heat the remaining oil and the butter in a small frying pan and fry the breacrumbs until golden.

Add freshly cooked pasta to the large frying pan. Stir well to coat the pasta with the oil mixture. Cook for 2 minutes, stirring continuously. Stir in the toasted breadcrumbs. Transfer to a serving bowl and garnish with fresh parsley leaves.

VEAL AND MUSHROOM SAUCE

Serves 4

Preparation time: 15 minutes + 45 minutes soaking + 15 minutes cooking

10 g dried porcini mushrooms	
100 ml (3½ fl oz) warm water	
40 g (1½ oz) butter	
500 g (1 lb) veal escalopes, sliced into thin strips	
2 tablespoons seasoned flour	

This wonderful sauce is one I always try to order in Italian restaurants. It is truly inspired! I love it with tagliarini or tagliatelle verdi.

Soak the porcini in the warm water for 45 minutes. Drain through muslin, reserving the soaking liquid. Rinse and slice thinly.

Melt the butter in a frying pan. Toss the veal strips in the seasoned flour and cook them in the butter for about 3 minutes until browned.

2 shallots, chopped finely

125 g (4 oz) chestnut
mushrooms, sliced thinly

1 teaspoon crushed green
peppercorns in brine

3 tablespoons dry white
wine

3 tablespoons crème fraîche
or double cream

½ teaspoon Worcestershire
sauce

juice of ½ lemon

4 tablespoons finely
chopped fresh parsley

salt and pepper

Remove the meat from the pan with a slotted spoon and drain on kitchen paper.

Add the shallots, the porcini and chestnut mushrooms and the peppercorns to the frying pan and fry for 3 minutes over a medium heat, stirring frequently. Add the wine and the porcini soaking liquid and cook until reduced by half. Add the crème fraîche or double cream and bring to the boil. Stir in the Worcestershire sauce and lemon juice. Return the veal to the pan and heat through. Adjust the seasoning and stir in the chopped parsley. Serve with freshly cooked pasta.

RAGÙ ALLA BOLOGNESE

Bolognese sauce	Serves 4

Preparation time: 15 minutes + 1 hour soaking + 1¾ hours cooking

10 g dried porcini
mushrooms

200 ml (7 fl oz) warm
water

50 g (2 oz) butter

1 small onion, chopped
finely

1 celery stick, chopped
finely

1 carrot, chopped finely

65 g (2½ oz) smoked
streaky bacon, chopped
finely

1 bay leaf

300 g (10 oz) minced beef

7 g (¼ oz) plain flour

125 ml (4 fl oz) red wine

1 pinch of grated nutmeg

True bolognese sauce does not contain tomatoes; tomatoes have been added over the years in other countries, as they shorten the cooking time. The traditional cooking time is typically around 2 hours, which makes this one of the longer pasta sauces to cook. The result is a sensational sauce, known as a ragù in Italy, similar to a stew. It goes well with all types of pasta, particularly spaghetti.

Soak the porcini mushrooms in the warm water for 1 hour.

In a large saucepan melt the butter and gently fry the onion, celery, carrot, bacon and bay leaf for 10 minutes, stirring frequently. Add the minced beef and cook until browned. Sprinkle in the flour, stir well to coat the meat and vegetables and cook for 30 seconds. Pour in the wine and stir over a high heat until most of it has evaporated.

Drain the porcini through muslin, reserving the soaking liquid. Rinse and finely chop the

125 ml (4 fl oz) beef stock
125 ml (4 fl oz) milk
4 tablespoons chopped fresh parsley, preferably flat-leaf
2 tablespoons single cream
salt and pepper
To garnish:
40 g (1½ oz) fresh parmesan cheese, sliced
fresh parsley sprigs

porcini. Add the porcini and the reserved liquid to the meat mixture. Add the nutmeg, seasoning and half the stock. Simmer for 1 hour, stirring at 15-minute intervals and topping up with the remaining stock as necessary.

Stir in the milk and simmer for 30 minutes. Stir in the chopped parsley and cream and adjust the seasoning. Remove the bay leaf. Serve with freshly cooked pasta, garnished with slices of parmesan cheese and parsley sprigs.

VEAL, WINE AND PEA SAUCE

Serves 4

Preparation time: 20 minutes + 25 minutes cooking

150 g (5 oz) frozen petits pois
375 g (12 oz) veal escalopes, cut into thin strips
3 tablespoons seasoned flour
50 g (2 oz) butter
2 shallots, chopped finely
1 tablespoon tomato purée
1 tablespoon chopped fresh sage
125 ml (4 fl oz) dry white wine
230 g (8 oz) can of chopped tomatoes, drained
125 ml (4 fl oz) chicken stock
salt and pepper
fresh sage leaves, to garnish

This is a variation of the classic Roman prosciutto and pea sauce using veal instead of prosciutto. It is traditionally served with paglia e fieno pasta.

Cook the peas in a small pan of salted boiling water for 2 minutes. Drain.

Coat the veal pieces in the seasoned flour. Melt the butter in a frying pan and cook for 2–3 minutes until the veal is browned. Remove the veal with a slotted spoon and keep warm.

Add the shallots to the pan and cook for about 5 minutes until softened. Add the tomato purée, sage, wine, tomatoes and chicken stock to the pan and cook for about 15 minutes until thickened.

Return the veal to the pan and adjust the seasoning. Stir in the peas. Toss the sauce with freshly cooked pasta and garnish with fresh sage leaves.

Veal, Wine and Pea Sauce
Ragù alla Bolognese (Bolognese sauce)

CACCIATORA SAUCE

Serves 4

Preparation time: 25 minutes + 20–25 minutes cooking

2 tablespoons olive oil

500 g (1 lb) pork fillet, cubed

1 onion, chopped

2 garlic cloves, chopped

1 celery stick, chopped

1 carrot, sliced

125 g (4 oz) button mushrooms

397 g (14 oz) can of chopped tomatoes, drained

2 tablespoons chopped fresh rosemary

1 teaspoon chopped fresh basil

1 teaspoon chopped fresh oregano

salt and pepper

fresh herbs, to garnish

Cacciatora *means 'cooked the hunter's way'. It is a popular sauce to cook in the autumn when mushrooms are abundant and may be served with tagliatelle or linguine.*

Heat the oil in a large saucepan and add the meat. Season well and cook for 3 minutes until evenly browned. Remove the meat from the pan with a slotted spoon.

Add the onion, garlic, celery and carrot to the pan and cook, stirring, for 5 minutes. Add the pork and the remaining ingredients. Stir well, cover and simmer for 15 minutes, stirring occasionally. Serve with freshly cooked pasta. Garnish with fresh herbs.

GORGONZOLA SAUCE

Serves 4

Preparation time: 5 minutes + 5 minutes cooking

50 g (2 oz) butter

2 garlic cloves, halved

50 g (2 oz) shelled pistachio nuts

200 g (7 oz) Gorgonzola cheese, crumbled

4 tablespoons milk

4 tablespoons double cream

Gorgonzola, an Italian blue-veined cow's milk cheese, is rich and creamy. Dolcelatte cheese can be substituted for the Gorgonzola if you prefer a milder blue cheese. This sauce is lovely with tagliatelle verdi.

Melt the butter in a non-stick saucepan and add the garlic and pistachios. Cook for 2 minutes, stirring. Remove the garlic and discard.

Add the Gorgonzola and milk to the saucepan

4 tablespoons grated
parmesan cheese

4 tablespoons chopped fresh
parsley, preferably flat-leaf

salt and pepper

fresh parsley sprigs, to
garnish

and stir for about 1 minute until the cheese
melts and the sauce is creamy. Adjust the
seasoning. Remove the pan from the heat and
stir in the double cream. Reheat briefly,
without boiling.

Toss the sauce with freshly cooked pasta, the
parmesan cheese and parsley. Serve garnished
with fresh parsley sprigs.

BACON AND CHEESE SAUCE

Serves 4

Preparation time: 15 minutes + 10 minutes cooking

1 small onion, chopped
finely

25 g (1 oz) butter

2 tablespoons plain flour

350 ml (12 fl oz) milk,
warmed

25 g (1 oz) Gruyère
cheese, grated finely

25 g (1 oz) parmesan
cheese, grated finely

5 streaky bacon rashers,
cooked and chopped

salt and pepper

*Serve with tagliatelle or fettuccine, a fresh green
salad and garlic bread for a terrific family meal.*

Fry the onion in the butter in a saucepan for
5 minutes, until softened. Stir in the flour and
cook for 2 minutes. Remove the pan from the
heat and add the warmed milk, whisking
continuously. Return the pan to the heat and
continue stirring until the mixture thickens.
Simmer the sauce for 5 minutes, stirring
frequently.

Strain the sauce through a fine sieve into a
serving bowl. Add the Gruyère, parmesan and
salt and pepper and toss well. Stir in the cooked
bacon. Serve with freshly cooked pasta.

Variation: Use a good farmhouse Cheddar
instead of the Gruyère cheese for a more tangy
flavour.

MUSHROOM AND TOMATO SAUCE

Serves 4

Preparation time: 20 minutes + 25 minutes cooking

40 g (1½ oz) butter

1 tablespoon olive oil

2–3 shallots, chopped
finely

*This sauce can be made with just about any
mushrooms. I particularly like a combination of
oyster and shiitake mushrooms. Serve it with
spaghetti or tagliarini.*

375 g (12 oz) assorted mushrooms, sliced	Heat the butter and olive oil in a saucepan and fry the shallots over a low heat for about 5 minutes until softened, stirring frequently. Increase the heat and add the mushrooms. Cook over a high heat, stirring, until golden in colour.
125 ml (4 fl oz) dry white wine	
397 g (14 oz) can of chopped tomatoes, drained	
2 garlic cloves, crushed	Add the white wine and boil until reduced by half. Stir in the tomatoes, garlic and double cream. Reduce the heat and simmer for 5 minutes.
3 tablespoons double cream	
2 tablespoons chopped fresh parsley	Remove the pan from the heat and stir in the parsley. Adjust the seasoning. Serve with freshly cooked pasta.
salt and pepper	

SARDINE SAUCE

Serves 4

Preparation time: 20 minutes + 20 minutes cooking

25 g (1 oz) fresh breadcrumbs	*This is a popular Sicilian dish, as sardines are fished in abundance off the coast. There is nothing like fresh sardines. Signs of freshness are a firm body and bright, clear eyes. Serve this sauce with tagliatelle verdi or tagliarini.*
50 g (2 oz) pine kernels	
125 ml (4 fl oz) olive oil	
1 small onion, chopped finely	
25 g (1 oz) raisins, soaked for 5 minutes and drained	Preheat the oven to Gas Mark 4/180°C/350°F or preheat the grill. Spread the breadcrumbs and pine kernels on a baking sheet and toast for 4–5 minutes until golden in colour.
2 tablespoons chopped fresh parsley	
8 fresh sardines weighing 750 g (1½ lb) in total, gutted	Heat half the oil in a large frying pan. Gently fry the onion for about 5 minutes until transparent. Remove the pan from the heat and stir in the breadcrumbs, pine kernels, drained raisins and parsley.
2 garlic cloves, sliced in half	
flour for dusting	Remove the heads and tails from the sardines (1). Open the fish out gently with your fingers and remove the bones (2).

Heat the remaining oil in a large frying pan. Add the garlic and cook until golden. Remove the garlic from the pan and discard. Lightly dust the sardines with flour and fry for 3 minutes, until golden. Gently turn over the fish and fry for a further 3 minutes.

Using a fish slice, transfer the sardines to the pan with the onions. Warm through. Adjust

salt and pepper

the seasoning before serving. Serve with freshly cooked pasta.

SALSA PICCANTE

Piquant sauce   Serves 4

Preparation time: 5 minutes + 20–25 minutes cooking

2 tablespoons olive oil

1 onion, sliced

397 g (14 oz) can of chopped tomatoes

2 teaspoons chopped fresh sage

2 teaspoons chopped fresh oregano

a pinch of chilli powder

3 tablespoons drained capers

2 tablespoons red wine vinegar

salt and pepper

The capers and vinegar give this sweet-and-sour sauce its piquancy – guaranteed to wake up a jaded palate! Try it with spaghetti.

Heat the olive oil in a frying pan over a low heat and fry the onion for about 5 minutes until softened, stirring frequently. Add the tomatoes and bring to the boil. Cook over a medium heat for 15–20 minutes until thickened.

Remove the pan from the heat and stir in the remaining ingredients. Adjust the seasoning and serve with freshly cooked pasta.

PUTTANESCA SAUCE

(Pictured on page 4 and on back cover)   Serves 4

Preparation time: 15 minutes + 30 minutes soaking + 10 minutes cooking

100 ml (3½ fl oz) olive oil

2 garlic cloves, crushed

This delicious sauce, usually served with spaghetti, originated in the red-light district of Naples. It is named after the ladies of easy virtue that inhabit these areas, hence its spiciness!

a pinch of dried crushed
chillies

6 anchovy fillets, drained
and soaked in milk for 30
minutes

400 g (14 oz) can of peeled
tomatoes

100 g (3½ oz) black
olives, pitted and sliced

1 tablespoon capers

1 teaspoon finely chopped
fresh oregano

1 tablespoon chopped fresh
parsley, preferably flat-leaf

fresh herbs, to garnish

Heat the olive oil in a heavy-based saucepan and
gently fry the garlic and chilli. Drain the
anchovies and add to the pan, mashing them up
whilst stirring.

Slit the tomatoes one by one over a bowl to
drain out some of the seeds and juice. Add the
tomatoes and can juices to the pan. Add the
olives, capers, oregano and parsley and cook
over a medium heat, stirring occasionally, for
10 minutes.

Pour the sauce over freshly cooked pasta and
sprinkle with fresh herbs.

MUSHROOM SAUCE WITH ANCHOVIES

Serves 4

Preparation time: 15 minutes + 25 minutes cooking

6 tablespoons olive oil

15 g (½ oz) butter

3 shallots, chopped finely

4 garlic cloves, chopped

500 g (1 lb) button
mushrooms

6 tablespoons dry white
wine

4 anchovy fillets, chopped

230 g (8 oz) can of chopped
tomatoes, drained

3 tablespoons chopped fresh
parsley

pepper

*I keep cans of anchovies on hand in the kitchen
cupboard, as they quickly transform the mild flavour
of cultivated mushrooms into a delicious sauce. Be
careful not to let the anchovies burn, however, or
they become unpleasantly bitter. This sauce is perfect
with garlic and herb tagliatelle.*

Heat the olive oil and butter in a frying pan and
gently fry the shallots and garlic for about
5 minutes until softened. Stir in the
mushrooms and cook, stirring frequently, for 5
minutes. Increase the heat, add the wine and
cook, stirring, until most of the wine has
evaporated. Stir in the anchovy pieces and
tomatoes and continue cooking over a high
heat, stirring frequently, for about 5–10
minutes until the sauce thickens.

Remove the pan from the heat and stir in the
parsley and pepper to taste. Serve with freshly
cooked pasta.

MEAT AND FISH SAUCES

SMOKED SALMON SAUCE

Serves 4

Preparation time: 5 minutes + 10 minutes cooking

50 g (2 oz) butter

2 shallots, chopped finely

284 ml (½ pint) carton of double cream

125 g (4 oz) smoked salmon, sliced into thin strips

3 tablespoons finely chopped fresh dill

salt and pepper

fresh dill sprigs, to garnish

This dish – completed with a mixture of egg and tagliatelle verdi – is perfect for a luncheon party. Delicious with a green salad and a chilled fruity white wine.

Melt the butter in a frying pan. Gently fry the shallots for about 3 minutes, until softened. Pour in the cream and warm through. Stir in the salmon strips and dill and cook over a low heat for 5 minutes. Taste and adjust the seasoning.

Toss the sauce with freshly cooked pasta. Garnish with fresh dill sprigs and serve.

ANCHOVY AND ROCKET SAUCE

Serves 4

Preparation time: 5 minutes + 5 minutes cooking

2 tablespoons olive oil

1 garlic clove, chopped

2 × 50 g (2 oz) can of anchovy fillets, drained and chopped

3 tablespoons dry white wine

25 g (1 oz) rocket leaves, shredded

2 tablespoons chopped fresh parsley

pepper

This sauce goes well with capellini.

Heat the olive oil in a frying pan and fry the garlic and anchovies for 3 minutes. Add the wine and cook, stirring, for 2 minutes. Remove the pan from the heat and stir in the rocket and parsley. Sprinkle the mixture generously with pepper and serve with freshly cooked pasta.

PRAWN AND MANGE TOUT SAUCE

Serves 4

Preparation time: 15 minutes + 5–10 minutes cooking

150 g (5 oz) mange tout,
topped and tailed

25 g (1 oz) butter

2 tablespoons olive oil

2.5 cm (1-inch) piece of
fresh root ginger, grated
finely

1 garlic clove, crushed

375 g (12 oz) peeled
prawns, thawed if frozen

150 g (5 oz) bean sprouts

juice of 1 lemon

1 tablespoon chopped fresh
dill

salt and pepper

fresh dill sprigs, to garnish

Meathalls in
Tomato
Sauce

Prawn and
Mange Tout
Sauce

Pork Paprikash Sauce

The ginger and bean sprouts give this sauce a delicate Far Eastern flavour. I would choose Venetian shells or conchiglie to extend the fish theme, but paglia e fieno is equally good.

Cook the mange tout in boiling salted water for 1 minute. Drain. Refresh with cold water and dry thoroughly on kitchen paper.

Heat the butter and oil in a frying pan. Fry the ginger and garlic for 2 minutes, until softened. Add the prawns and cook for 1–2 minutes, stirring frequently. Add the bean sprouts and mange tout and cover. Cook for about 1 minute until heated through. Remove the pan from the heat and stir in the lemon juice and dill.

Stir the sauce into freshly cooked pasta and sprinkle with pepper. Serve garnished with dill sprigs.

PORK PAPRIKASH SAUCE

Serves 4

Preparation time: 20 minutes + 20 minutes cooking

2 tablespoons plain flour
1 tablespoon paprika
½ teaspoon salt
¼ teaspoon pepper
500 g (1 lb) pork fillet, cubed
3 tablespoons olive oil
1 onion, chopped
1 celery stick, chopped
1 green pepper, de-seeded and sliced
2 × 397 g (14 oz) can of chopped tomatoes with herbs
142 ml (5 fl oz) carton of soured cream, at room temperature, to serve

Try this with a hollow pasta shape such as penne rigate which will absorb the sauce.

Combine the flour, paprika, salt and pepper in a mixing bowl. Add the pork pieces and mix well to coat.

In a heavy-based saucepan, heat 2 tablespoons of the oil. Add the pork and fry until browned on all sides. Remove the pork with a slotted spoon and keep warm.

Add the remaining oil to the saucepan and cook the onion, celery and green pepper for 5 minutes, stirring. Return the pork pieces to the pan and stir in the chopped tomatoes. Cook, uncovered, for 20 minutes, stirring occasionally.

Serve the sauce with freshly cooked pasta and the soured cream.

MEATBALLS IN TOMATO SAUCE

Serves 6

Preparation time: 20 minutes + 25–30 minutes cooking

375 g (12 oz) minced pork
375 g (12 oz) minced beef
4 tablespoons chopped fresh parsley, preferably flat-leaf
1 garlic clove, chopped finely
15 g (½ oz) parmesan cheese, grated finely
40 g (1½ oz) breadcrumbs
1 egg

A real childhood favourite. Try doubling the quantities and freezing half for another day. It is usually served with spaghetti.

In a mixing bowl combine the meat, parsley, garlic, parmesan, breadcrumbs, seasoning and egg. With wet fingers, shape the mixture into balls the size of large walnuts.

Heat the oil in a frying pan and fry the meatballs for at least 10 minutes, until well browned. Lift out the meatballs with a slotted spoon.

2 tablespoons olive oil

2 quantities of Pommarola (Neapolitan tomato sauce, page 12) or a 550 g (1 lb 2 oz) jar of Classic Italian Sauce

salt and pepper

To garnish and serve:

grated parmesan cheese

fresh parsley sprigs

Drain the fat from the pan, add the tomato sauce and return the meatballs. Bring to the boil and then reduce to a simmer. Simmer, covered, for 15–20 minutes. Serve with freshly cooked pasta and grated parmesan cheese and garnish with fresh parsley sprigs.

SPICY GROUND TURKEY SAUCE

(Pictured on page 5)   Serves 4

Preparation time: 10 minutes + 20 minutes cooking

4 tablespoons olive oil

1 red onion, chopped finely

2 garlic cloves, chopped finely

1 red pepper, de-seeded and chopped

1 teaspoon chilli powder

1/2 teaspoon ground cumin

1/4 teaspoon Cayenne pepper

500 g (1 lb) minced turkey

397 g (14 oz) can of chopped tomatoes

pinch of dried crushed chillies

25 g (1 oz) fresh coriander leaves, chopped finely

salt and pepper

fresh coriander leaves, to garnish

The spices in this sauce are all popular in dishes from the south-west American states. It looks particularly attractive with fusilli tricolori.

Heat the oil in a large frying pan and fry the onion for about 5 minutes until softened. Add the garlic, red pepper and spices and cook for 1 minute.

Stir in the minced turkey and cook for 3–4 minutes, until the turkey is no longer pink. Stir in the tomatoes, crushed chillies and chopped coriander and adjust the seasoning. Simmer the sauce for 10 minutes, stirring occasionally.

Toss the sauce with freshly cooked pasta and garnish with fresh coriander leaves.

Variation: Drain a 432 g (15 oz) can of red kidney beans and stir the beans into the sauce for the last 5 minutes of cooking.

CREAMY SPINACH AND PROSCIUTTO SAUCE

Serves 4–6

Preparation time: 10 minutes + 10 minutes cooking

284 ml (½ pint) carton of double cream

50 g (2 oz) butter

75 g (3 oz) prosciutto crudo, sliced into long, thin strips

250 g (8 oz) fresh spinach, stalks removed, cut into long, thin strips

freshly grated parmesan cheese, to serve

Definitely not a sauce for weight watchers! The cream makes it very rich and filling, perfect as a main course served with paglia e fieno.

In a small saucepan gently boil the cream for about 5 minutes until it is reduced by half.

Melt the butter in a frying pan and cook the prosciutto strips for 1 minute. Add the spinach and cook for about 3 minutes until soft.

Toss the cream and the spinach mixture with freshly cooked pasta. Serve with freshly grated parmesan cheese.

MUSSEL, SPINACH AND LEEK SAUCE

Serves 4

Preparation time: 20 minutes + 25–30 minutes cooking

1 kg (2 lb) fresh mussels

65 g (2½ oz) butter

2 shallots, chopped finely

3 large leeks, cut into long, thin strips

375 g (12 oz) fresh spinach, stems removed, cut into long, thin strips

½ × 400 g (14 oz) can of pimientos, drained and sliced into long, thin strips

salt and pepper

Mussels are said to be at their best during months with the letter 'r' in them. This is an attractive sauce which looks pretty with farfalle, and it is ideal for entertaining. I like to serve it as a starter with a bottle of crisp white wine.

Discard any mussels that are open and do not close when tapped sharply on the work surface. Scrub the closed mussels under cold running water and remove the beards. Put the mussels in a heavy pan, cover and cook (without liquid) over a high heat for 5 minutes, shaking the pan occasionally, until they open. Discard any that do not open. Strain the liquid through muslin and reserve. Remove most of the mussels from their shells, reserving a few in their shells to garnish.

Transfer the strained cooking liquid to a small saucepan and boil rapidly until reduced by half.

Mussel, Spinach and Leek Sauce
Creamy Spinach and Prosciutto Sauce

36

Melt the butter in a frying pan and gently cook the shallots for 5 minutes, stirring. Add the leeks and spinach, season well and cook for 10 minutes. Stir in the pimiento strips, shelled mussels and reduced cooking liquid. Cook for 3 minutes and then adjust the seasoning.

Toss the sauce with freshly cooked pasta and garnish with the reserved mussels in their shells.

BAKED BEAN AND SAUSAGE SAUCE

Serves 4

Preparation time: 5 minutes + 35–40 minutes cooking

4 tablespoons olive oil

2 garlic cloves, sliced in half lengthways

1 small onion, sliced

250 g (8 oz) pork sausages, sliced

397 g (14 oz) can of chopped tomatoes

447 g (15 oz) can of beans in tomato sauce

1 Peperami stick, sliced thinly

1/4 teaspoon dried crushed chillies

125 ml (4 fl oz) water

pepper

This sauce is a winner with both adults and children, as it combines two childhood favourites. It is perfect with rigatoni for a Sunday evening meal. Any leftover sauce tastes delicious on toast.

Heat the oil in a large saucepan and fry the garlic until golden. Remove the garlic with a slotted spoon and discard.

Add the onion and sausage slices to the pan and fry gently for 5–10 minutes, until cooked through.

Drain the oil from the pan. Stir in the tomatoes, beans in tomato sauce, Peperami slices, crushed chillies and water. Bring to the boil, reduce the heat and simmer for 20–25 minutes, stirring occasionally. Season with pepper. Serve with freshly cooked pasta.

CHICKEN SAUCE WITH MARSALA

Serves 4

Preparation time: 10 minutes + 25–30 minutes cooking

5 tablespoons olive oil

1 small onion, chopped

2 garlic cloves, chopped

500 g (1 lb) boneless, skinless chicken breasts, cut into strips

125 g (4 oz) smoked streaky bacon, chopped

5 tablespoons Marsala

397 g (14 oz) can of chopped tomatoes

salt and pepper

Marsala is a fortified Italian wine made in Sicily. It adds a subtle sweetness to this sauce, which is lovely served with a mixture of egg tagliatelle and tagliatelle verdi.

Heat the olive oil in a saucepan and fry the onion and garlic for 5 minutes, stirring until softened.

Increase the heat to moderate and add the chicken and bacon. Cook, stirring, until golden. Add the Marsala and cook, stirring, until it reduces by half. Stir in the tomatoes and bring to a boil. Reduce the heat to a simmer and cook for 15–20 minutes until thickened, stirring frequently. Season to taste and serve with freshly cooked pasta.

CRAB AND PESTO SAUCE

Serves 4

Preparation time: 10 minutes + 5 minutes cooking

25 g (1 oz) butter

50 g (2 oz) shiitake or oyster mushrooms, sliced

1/2 quantity of Pesto (Basil sauce, page 18)

1 large tomato, skinned, de-seeded and chopped coarsely

zest of 1/2 lemon

250 g (8 oz) fresh or canned white and/or brown crab meat

salt and pepper

Try this sauce with a long pasta such as capellini.

Melt the butter in a large frying pan over a medium heat. Add the mushrooms and fry for about 3 minutes until tender. Mix in the Pesto, tomato and lemon zest. Stir in the crab meat and cook until just heated through. Taste and adjust the seasoning.

Serve the sauce with freshly cooked pasta.

SMOKED TROUT AND FISH ROE SAUCE WITH CHIVES

Serves 4

Preparation time: 5 minutes + 5 minutes cooking

300 ml (½ pint) crème fraîche or double cream

2 tablespoons chopped fresh dill

2 tablespoons chopped fresh chives

250 g (8 oz) smoked trout, flaked

To garnish:

½ × 100 g (3½ oz) jar of red lumpfish caviar

½ × 100 g (3½ oz) jar of black lumpfish caviar

fresh dill sprigs

Save this luxurious sauce for an extra-special occasion, such as New Year's eve or an intimate dinner party, because it is rather extravagant. The stunning colours look wonderful with egg tagliatelle or linguine.

In a saucepan bring the crème fraîche or double cream to the boil. Cook for about 5 minutes until reduced by half. Stir in the dill, chives and trout and remove the pan from the heat.

Mix the trout sauce carefully with freshly cooked pasta. Serve garnished with the red and black lumpfish caviar and fresh dill sprigs.

SMOKED SALMON AND ASPARAGUS SAUCE

Serves 4–6

Preparation time: 20 minutes + 5–10 minutes cooking

500 g (1 lb) asparagus spears, trimmed and cut diagonally into 2.5 cm (1-inch) pieces

50 g (2 oz) unsalted butter

250 g (8 oz) sliced smoked salmon, cut into strips

284 ml (½ pint) carton of double cream

thinly grated zest of ½ lemon

This sauce combines my two favourite luxury ingredients. Try to use sprue or thin asparagus rather than the thick variety. If you prefer the thick variety, simply give it a good scrape with a vegetable peeler before cooking and discard any woody stems. This is lovely with tagliatelle or tagliarini.

Steam the asparagus for about 5 minutes, until just tender. Drain and refresh in cold water. Dry thoroughly on kitchen paper.

In a frying pan melt the butter and gently fry

Smoked Salmon and Asparagus Sauce
Smoked Trout and Fish Roe Sauce with Chives

a squeeze of lemon juice

pepper

lemon slices, to garnish

the salmon strips for 30 seconds. Add the cream and lemon zest and juice and heat gently, stirring, until just heated through. Stir in the asparagus pieces and remove from the heat. Season with pepper.

Toss the sauce with freshly cooked pasta and garnish with lemon slices.

LEBANESE LAMB AND SPINACH SAUCE

Serves 4

Preparation time: 10 minutes + 20–25 minutes cooking

500 g (1 lb) frozen spinach, thawed

50 g (2 oz) onion, chopped

2 tablespoons vegetable oil

1 teaspoon ground cumin

1/2 teaspoon ground coriander

a generous pinch of ground cinnamon

500 g (1 lb) boned shoulder of lamb, cubed

1 large garlic clove

1/4 teaspoon salt

300 ml (1/2 pint) greek-style yogurt

1 tablespoon chopped fresh mint

fresh mint leaves, to garnish

The spices in this sauce – good served with tagliatelle verdi – give it a typically Middle Eastern flavour. Try serving it with grilled pitta bread and mint tea for authenticity!

Squeeze as much water as possible out of the spinach with your hands. Cook the spinach, without water, in a saucepan. Boil until most of the liquid has evaporated, stirring frequently.

In another saucepan fry the onion in the oil for 5 minutes. Add the spices and cook for 1 minute. Add the lamb pieces and toss to coat well with the spices. Cook the lamb for 5–10 minutes, or until done to your liking. Add the spinach and mix well. Cook for 1 minute.

In a small saucepan boil the garlic in boiling water for 5 minutes. Remove the garlic with a slotted spoon and mash to a paste with the salt. Stir into the yogurt, along with the chopped mint.

Mix the yogurt sauce with the meat and spinach mixture. Serve with freshly cooked pasta and garnish with fresh mint leaves.

CHICKEN LIVER AND GREEN BEAN SAUCE

Serves 4

Preparation time: 10 minutes + 15 minutes cooking

250 g (8 oz) green beans, halved

1½ tablespoons corn oil

25 g (1 oz) butter

300 g (10 oz) chicken livers, thawed if frozen, halved

1 teaspoon balsamic vinegar

125 ml (4 fl oz) chicken stock

2 tablespoons shredded fresh sage leaves

salt and pepper

Balsamic vinegar is an exquisite aged vinegar from Italy. It has a sweet-and-sour flavour that is unmistakable. It seems to bring out all the flavours of the chicken livers in this sauce, which goes well with egg tagliatelle.

Bring a saucepan of salted water to the boil and blanch the beans for 1 minute. Rinse in cold water and drain on kitchen paper.

Heat the oil and butter in a large frying pan and add the chicken livers. Season well and cook over a moderate heat for 1–2 minutes until well browned. Remove the pan from the heat and add the balsamic vinegar, stirring well. Return to the heat. Pour in the stock, increase the heat and boil until reduced by half. Stir in the beans and sage. Adjust the seasoning and serve with freshly cooked pasta.

BROCCOLI AND ANCHOVY SAUCE

Serves 4

Preparation time: 20 minutes + 10–15 minutes cooking

500 g (1 lb) broccoli

3 garlic cloves, chopped

2 anchovy fillets, chopped finely

¼ teaspoon dried crushed chillies

6 tablespoons olive oil

4 tablespoons shredded fresh parsley, preferably flat-leaf

salt and pepper

The anchovies in this sauce literally melt when cooked and give it a delicious piquancy. Serve it with fusilli.

Trim the broccoli, separating the florets from the stalks. Thinly slice the stalks. Blanch the broccoli in a saucepan of boiling salted water for 3 minutes. Drain and rinse with cold water.

In a large frying pan fry the garlic, anchovies and chillies in the olive oil for 5 minutes.

Add the broccoli to the pan and cook, stirring, for 5 minutes. Stir in the parsley and season with salt and pepper. Serve with freshly cooked pasta.

CHICKEN AND ANCHOVY SAUCE

Preparation time: 20 minutes + about 15 minutes cooking

1 garlic clove, chopped

3 tablespoons olive oil

750 g (1½ lb) boneless, skinless chicken breasts, cut into 5 cm (2-inch) pieces

250 g (8 oz) green beans, cut into 5 cm (2-inch) pieces

1 red pepper, de-seeded and cut into thin strips

3 spring onions, sliced

4 plum tomatoes, skinned and quartered

50 g (2 oz) can of anchovy fillets, drained and chopped coarsely

juice of 1 lemon

salt and pepper

Even if you think you don't like anchovies, this sauce is guaranteed to convert you. The anchovies complement the chicken beautifully, giving the sauce, which is particularly good with vermicelli, richness and depth of flavour.

In a large saucepan cook the garlic in the oil for 1 minute. Add the chicken pieces and cook for 3 minutes, tossing well to coat in the oil.

Add the beans, red pepper and spring onions to the chicken and cook for 2 minutes.

Add the tomatoes and anchovies and cook for 5 minutes. Sprinkle with the lemon juice and adjust the seasoning. Cook for 2 minutes. Serve with freshly cooked pasta.

Chicken and Anchovy Sauce
Mediterranean Cod Sauce

MEDITERRANEAN COD SAUCE

(Pictured also on front cover)   Serves 4

Preparation time: 20 minutes + 30–35 minutes cooking

1 onion, chopped
1 green pepper, de-seeded and chopped
1 celery stick, chopped
2 tablespoons vegetable oil
1 garlic clove, chopped
450 ml (¾ pint) fish stock
397 g (14 oz) can of chopped tomatoes
a pinch of Cayenne pepper
750 g (1½ lb) cod fillet, skinned and cut into 2.5 cm (1-inch) pieces
salt and pepper

This sauce looks particularly pretty served on conchiglie.

In a large saucepan cook the onion, green pepper and celery in the oil for 5 minutes. Add the garlic and cook, stirring, for 1 minute.

Stir in the stock, tomatoes and Cayenne pepper and bring to the boil. Boil, uncovered, for 20–25 minutes, stirring occasionally until thickened.

Add the cod and seasoning to the pan and cook over a low heat for 5 minutes. Check and adjust the seasoning. Serve spooned over freshly cooked pasta.

TUNA NIÇOISE SAUCE

                                                                 Serves 4

Preparation time: 15 minutes

198 g (7 oz) can of tuna in brine, drained
75 g (3 oz) black olives, pitted
50 g (2 oz) can of anchovies, drained
4 tablespoons capers
1 tablespoon fresh lemon juice
50 ml (2 fl oz) extra-virgin olive oil
1 tablespoon brandy
pepper

I adored tuna as a child and it is still one of my favourite foods. This sauce is easy to make and you will probably find, like me, that you can never make enough. Serve it with hot spaghetti.

Combine the tuna, olives, anchovies and capers in a blender or food processor and blend to a thick paste.

With the motor running, drizzle in the lemon juice and olive oil to form a thick paste. Add the brandy and a generous grinding of black pepper. Check the seasoning. Serve mixed into hot pasta.

COURGETTE AND PROSCIUTTO SAUCE

Serves 4

Preparation time: 10 minutes + 20 minutes cooking

50 g (2 oz) butter

125 g (4 oz) prosciutto crudo, chopped

1 small onion, chopped

500 g (1 lb) courgettes, sliced

50 g (2 oz) crème fraîche or double cream

75 g (3 oz) parmesan cheese, grated finely

salt and pepper

Prosciutto, also known as Parma ham, is a type of cured ham. The curing process takes about 14 months. Prosciutto has a slightly sweet flavour and is always served in paper-thin slices. I like this sauce with capellini.

Melt the butter in a frying pan over a moderate heat and cook the prosciutto, stirring, for 2–3 minutes. Remove the prosciutto from the pan with a slotted spoon and drain on kitchen paper.

Add the onion to the pan and fry gently, stirring, for 5 minutes. Add the courgette slices and cook, stirring frequently, for 5–10 minutes until softened.

Return the prosciutto to the pan and stir in the crème fraîche or double cream and parmesan. Season to taste and serve with freshly cooked pasta.

TOMATO SAUCE WITH TUNA

Serves 4

Preparation time: 5 minutes + 20 minutes cooking

4 tablespoons olive oil

1 small onion, chopped

2 garlic cloves, chopped

40 g (1½ oz) black olives, pitted and chopped

397 g (14 oz) can of chopped tomatoes

198 g (7 oz) can of tuna, drained and flaked

2 teaspoons chopped fresh oregano or 1 teaspoon dried marjoram

Try serving this delicious sauce with conchiglie.

Heat the olive oil in a saucepan and fry the onion and garlic for about 5 minutes until softened.

Stir in the olives and tomatoes and cook, stirring frequently, for 15 minutes until thickened.

Stir in the tuna and oregano or marjoram. Heat through for 1 minute, then remove the pan from the heat. Serve with freshly cooked pasta.

MINCED MEAT AND PEA SAUCE

Serves 4

Preparation time: 15 minutes + 1 hour 10 minutes cooking

3 tablespoons olive oil

1 carrot, chopped

1 onion, chopped finely

1 tablespoon chopped fresh parsley

500 g (1 lb) minced beef or lamb

1 tablespoon plain flour

125 ml (4 fl oz) red wine

397 g (14 oz) can of chopped tomatoes, drained

250 ml (8 fl oz) chicken stock

125 g (4 oz) mushrooms, sliced

150 g (5 oz) frozen peas, thawed

salt and pepper

This sauce is a variation of Ragù alla Bolognese (Bolognese sauce, page 23) and also goes well with spaghetti. Unlike authentic bolognese, this sauce contains tomatoes.

Heat the olive oil in a saucepan and fry the carrot, onion and parsley for about 5 minutes until softened. Add the minced meat and cook until browned, stirring frequently.

Sprinkle over the flour and stir well to mix. Stir in the red wine and cook until reduced by half. Stir in the tomatoes, chicken stock and mushrooms and bring to the boil. Season well and reduce the heat to a simmer. Simmer for 1 hour, covered, stirring frequently. If the sauce is not sufficiently thickened after 1 hour, remove the cover, bring to the boil and cook until thickened.

Stir the peas into the sauce and cook for 1 minute. Season to taste and serve with freshly cooked pasta.

BACON AND SPINACH SAUCE

Serves 4

Preparation time: 10 minutes + 35–40 minutes cooking

25 g (1 oz) butter

2 shallots, chopped finely

500 g (1 lb) frozen leaf spinach, thawed

2 tablespoons olive oil

175 g (6 oz) streaky bacon, chopped

397 g (14 oz) can of chopped tomatoes, drained

Try this sauce with spaghetti or tagliarini.

In a frying pan melt the butter and add half the chopped shallots. Fry, stirring, for about 5 minutes until softened. Squeeze as much water as possible out of the spinach with your hands. Add the spinach to the frying pan and season well. Cook for 2 minutes over a medium heat, stirring constantly. Transfer the spinach mixture to a bowl and set aside.

Add the olive oil to the frying pan and fry the

2 tablespoons grated parmesan cheese

salt and pepper

remaining shallot for about 5 minutes until softened. Add the bacon and cook for 5 minutes, until golden brown. Stir in the tomatoes and cook over a moderate heat for 15–20 minutes until thickened.

Stir in the spinach and heat through. Adjust the seasoning. Remove the pan from the heat and stir in the parmesan. Serve with freshly cooked pasta.

PINK AND WHITE SEAFOOD SAUCE

Serves 4

Preparation time: 10 minutes + 15 minutes cooking

2 tablespoons sunflower oil

25 g (1 oz) butter

a bunch of spring onions, sliced

500 g (1 lb) monkfish, skinned and cut into 2.5 cm (1-inch) pieces

125 g (4 oz) peeled prawns, thawed if frozen

142 ml (¼ pint) carton of double cream

4 tablespoons chopped fresh parsley

salt and pepper

The texture and flavour of monkfish is similar to lobster, giving it the nickname of 'poor man's lobster'. Monkfish is simple to prepare. Before cooking remove the light membrane coating with a knife – it pulls away easily. I like to serve this attractive sauce with tagliatelle verdi.

Heat the oil and butter in a frying pan and gently fry the spring onions until softened. Stir in the monkfish and prawns and cook for 3–4 minutes until the monkfish is tender. Stir gently to prevent the fish sticking to the pan.

Stir in the cream and heat through for 1–2 minutes. Stir in the chopped parsley and adjust the seasoning. Serve with freshly cooked pasta.

SCALLOP SAUCE

Serves 4

Preparation time: 10 minutes + 10–15 minutes cooking

100 g (3½ oz) butter

2 shallots, chopped finely

40 g (1½ oz) chopped fresh parsley, preferably flat-leaf

125 ml (4 fl oz) dry white wine

500 g (1 lb) scallops with corals attached

250 g (8 oz) crème fraîche or double cream

125 g (4 oz) parmesan cheese, grated finely

2 tablespoons chopped fresh chives

a pinch of ground nutmeg

salt and white pepper

To garnish:

fresh parsley sprigs

fresh chives

Scallops are abundant and inexpensive in New England, on America's Atlantic coast, where I am from, but somewhat pricey here. Make this sauce when scallops are in season and serve it with paglia e fieno.

Melt the butter in a large frying pan. Fry the shallots and 3 tablespoons of the parsley for about 3 minutes, until softened. Add the wine and boil until reduced by half.

Add the scallops to the frying pan and cook for 1 minute. Remove the pan from the heat and stir in the crème fraîche or double cream. Stir in the parmesan, the remaining parsley, the chives and nutmeg. Taste and adjust the seasoning.

Toss the scallop mixture with freshly cooked pasta. Garnish with fresh parsley and chives and serve.

VEGETARIAN SAUCES

Some of the recipes in this chapter use non-vegetarian cheeses. However, there are a number of cheeses available that are suitable for vegetarians and these can be used instead if wished. These include vegetarian Cheddar cheese, which can be used as an alternative to parmesan and Gruyère, and many soft cheeses, such as cottage cheese, cream cheese, curd cheese, Danish blue and mozzarella. Some goat's milk and sheep's milk cheeses are also suitable.

SHIITAKE MUSHROOM AND SAGE SAUCE

Serves 4

Preparation time: 20 minutes + 45 minutes soaking + 20–25 minutes cooking

10 g dried porcini mushrooms

100 ml (3½ fl oz) warm water

50 g (2 oz) butter

2 shallots, chopped finely

400 g (13 oz) shiitake mushrooms, sliced

1 tablespoon finely chopped fresh sage

1 tablespoon finely chopped fresh parsley, preferably flat-leaf

4 tablespoons freshly grated parmesan cheese

salt and pepper

fresh sage leaves, to garnish

This sauce combines both Eastern and Western flavours: shiitake mushrooms are popular in Chinese and Japanese cookery and the porcini are typically Italian. The dried mushrooms give the sauce a woody depth of flavour which is truly delicious. Try serving it with paglia e fieno.

Soak the porcini in the water for 45 minutes. Drain through muslin, reserving the soaking liquid. Rinse and slice thinly.

Heat 15 g (½ oz) of the butter in a frying pan and gently fry the shallots for about 5 minutes until softened. Add the porcini and their soaking liquid and cook until the liquid evaporates. Add another 15 g (½ oz) of the butter, the shiitake mushrooms and the herbs. Season well and cook for 10 minutes.

Toss the sauce with freshly cooked pasta, the remaining butter and the parmesan. Garnish with fresh sage leaves and serve.

Coriander and Parsley
Pesto

Garlic Mushroom Sauce

GARLIC MUSHROOM SAUCE

Serves 4

Preparation time: 5 minutes + 15 minutes cooking

75 g (3 oz) butter

750 g (1½ lb) button mushrooms

juice of 1 lemon

3 garlic cloves, chopped

2 tablespoons chopped fresh parsley

salt and pepper

fresh parsley sprigs, to garnish

For an excellent variation on this sauce, use equal quantities of different mushrooms such as shiitake and oyster mushrooms. Serve it with farfalle.

Melt the butter in a heavy-based pan, add the mushrooms, cover and cook for 10 minutes, stirring occasionally.

Add the lemon juice and garlic to the mushrooms. Cover and cook for 5 minutes, stirring occasionally. Add the parsley, season with salt and pepper and mix well.

Serve the sauce with freshly cooked pasta and garnish with fresh parsley.

*Grilled Mediterranean
Vegetable Sauce*

CORIANDER AND PARSLEY PESTO

Serves 4

Preparation time: 5 minutes

1 small onion, chopped	
40 g (1½ oz) fresh coriander leaves	
50 g (2 oz) fresh parsley	
2 tablespoons red wine vinegar	
175 ml (6 fl oz) olive oil	
40 g (1½ oz) unsalted cashew nuts, chopped	
salt and pepper	

Try serving this variation of traditional basil-based pesto, with its extremely appetising green colour, with tortelloni or cappelletti.

In a blender or food processor combine the onion, coriander and parsley and blend to make a thick paste. With the motor running, drizzle in the vinegar and olive oil. Adjust the seasoning.

Transfer the pesto to a serving bowl and stir in the chopped cashews. Serve with freshly cooked pasta.

Variation: Use toasted walnuts or pine kernels instead of the cashews.

GRILLED MEDITERRANEAN VEGETABLE SAUCE

Serves 4

Preparation time: 15 minutes + 45 minutes cooking

1 aubergine, cut in half lengthways	
6 tablespoons olive oil	
1 large orange or yellow pepper	
2 extra large or 6–8 small tomatoes, skinned	
juice of 1 lemon	
4 tablespoons chopped fresh basil leaves	
salt and pepper	
fresh basil leaves, to garnish	

This sauce, delicious with vermicelli, may remind you of summer holidays! Although grilling peppers may seem tedious, the final result is worth it. Grilling brings out their rich, succulent flavour. Be sure to use extra-virgin olive oil.

Preheat the oven to Gas Mark 4/180°C/350°F. Brush the aubergine halves all over with 2 tablespoons of the olive oil. Lay them face down on an oiled baking sheet and roast for 45 minutes. Leave to cool.

Meanwhile, roast the pepper under a hot grill, turning frequently, until the skin is charred. Transfer the pepper to a plastic bag, seal the bag and leave to cool.

Cut large thin slices of flesh from the tomatoes and discard the centre, juice and seeds. Cut the flesh into 1 cm (½-inch) pieces.

Scoop out the flesh from the aubergine, discarding the skin. Chop the flesh roughly. Skin the pepper, remove the seeds and membrane and chop the flesh into 2.5 cm (1-inch) pieces. Combine the pepper in a bowl with the chopped tomatoes and aubergine. Toss with the remaining olive oil, the lemon juice and chopped basil. Season with salt and pepper.

Serve with freshly cooked pasta and garnish with fresh basil leaves.

FOUR-ONION SAUCE

Serves 4

Preparation time: 10 minutes + 40 minutes cooking

125 g (4 oz) butter

175 g (6 oz) red or spanish onions, sliced thinly

150 g (5 oz) spring onions, sliced thinly

150 g (5 oz) shallots, sliced thinly

150 ml (¼ pint) vegetable stock

200 ml (7 fl oz) double cream

a bunch of chives, chopped

25 g (1 oz) parmesan cheese, grated finely (optional)

salt and pepper

If you prefer a sweeter sauce, use red onions, which tend to be sweeter than the spanish variety. Equal quantities of the two gives a delightful mixture of sweet and sharp flavours, which is complemented by the more delicate flavours of the shallots and chives. I like to serve this with paglia e fieno.

Melt the butter in a heavy-based saucepan and add the onions and shallots. Fry gently for 15 minutes until softened, but not brown, stirring frequently. Pour over the stock and bring to the boil. Reduce the heat to a simmer and cover. Simmer for 25 minutes, stirring occasionally.

Stir in the double cream and chives. Season well. Heat through without boiling. Remove the pan from the heat and stir in the parmesan cheese, if using. Serve with freshly cooked pasta.

PEPERONATA

Preparation time: 15 minutes + 30 minutes cooking

2 red peppers

2 green peppers

2 orange or yellow peppers

175 ml (6 fl oz) olive oil

4 tablespoons red wine vinegar

25 g (1 oz) caster sugar

salt

I love serving this as a dinner party starter with tagliatelle because the colours are so pretty. If there's any left over, try it on bruschetta *(grilled Italian garlic toast).*

De-seed and slice the peppers into long strips.

Heat the oil in a heavy-based saucepan and add the peppers, tossing well to coat them in the oil. Simmer over a low heat, covered, for 30 minutes.

Remove the pan from the heat and stir in the vinegar, sugar, and salt to taste. Serve with freshly cooked pasta.

ROASTED RED PEPPER SAUCE

Preparation and cooking time: 25–30 minutes

4½ large red peppers, de-seeded and quartered

4 garlic cloves, chopped

125 g (4 oz) parmesan cheese, grated finely

4 tablespoons olive oil

salt and pepper

Roasting peppers in the oven is a good alternative to grilling them, and the results are just as good. This sauce looks lovely served on paglia e fieno or tagliatelle verdi.

Preheat the oven to Gas Mark 9/240°C/475°F. Place the pepper pieces on a baking sheet and roast in the oven for 20 minutes. Place them in a plastic bag, seal it and leave to cool. When cool enough to handle, remove the skins.

Reserve 2 of the pepper quarters and cut them into strips for the garnish. Purée the remaining peppers in a blender or food processor with the garlic and parmesan. With the motor running, add the oil. Taste and adjust the seasoning.

Serve with freshly cooked pasta and garnish with the reserved pepper strips.

Peperonata
Roasted Red Pepper Sauce

GUACAMOLE SAUCE

Preparation time: 10 minutes

4 ripe avocados, halved and pitted

1 small onion, chopped

150 ml (¼ pint) olive oil

juice of 2 lemons

1½ teaspoons salt

3 teaspoons chilli powder

1 extra large or 3–4 small tomatoes, skinned, de-seeded and cubed

142 ml (¼ pint) carton of soured cream, to serve

A real Mexican favourite, guacamole sauce, served with tagliatelle verdi, can easily be prepared year-round. Choose avocados which are just tender.

Combine all the ingredients, except the tomato and soured cream, in a food processor or blender and purée until smooth. Transfer the mixture to a mixing bowl and gently stir in the tomato.

Serve with freshly cooked pasta and spoon soured cream onto each portion.

MUSHROOM AND PEA SAUCE

Preparation time: 15 minutes + 15 minutes cooking

25 g (1 oz) butter

375 g (12 oz) chestnut or brown cap mushrooms, sliced

1 tablespoon plain flour

125 ml (4 fl oz) dry white wine

142 ml (¼ pint) carton of single cream

125 g (4 oz) shelled peas, thawed if frozen

salt and pepper

25 g (1 oz) parmesan cheese, grated finely, to serve

This sauce looks and tastes particularly good with fusilli tricolori.

Melt the butter in a frying pan over a low heat and fry the mushrooms, stirring frequently, for 5 minutes. Stir in the flour and mix well until all the butter is absorbed.

Stir in the wine and cook, stirring, until the sauce thickens. Stir in the cream and mix well. Add the peas and simmer until cooked. Adjust the seasoning.

Serve with freshly cooked pasta and the grated parmesan.

AUBERGINE AND CHEESE SAUCE

Serves 4

Preparation time: 15 minutes + 1 hour salting + 40 minutes cooking

500 g (1 lb) aubergines, peeled and cut into 2.5 cm (1-inch) cubes

3 tablespoons olive oil

2 garlic cloves, chopped

1 onion, chopped

1 carrot, chopped

1 celery stick, chopped

397 g (14 oz) can of chopped tomatoes, drained

2 tablespoons finely grated parmesan cheese

25 g (1 oz) ricotta cheese, crumbled

8 fresh basil leaves, shredded

salt and pepper

Salting aubergine releases its bitter juices which are then rinsed away before cooking. Try this sauce with wholewheat spirals.

Sprinkle the aubergine generously with salt and leave for at least 1 hour in a colander. Rinse well and pat dry with kitchen paper.

Heat the olive oil in a frying pan and gently fry the garlic, onion, carrot and celery for about 5 minutes until softened. Add the aubergine and cook, stirring, for 5 minutes. Add the chopped tomatoes and bring to the boil. Reduce the heat to a simmer and cover. Cook for 30 minutes, stirring occasionally.

Remove the pan from the heat and stir in the cheeses and basil. Adjust the seasoning. Serve with freshly cooked pasta.

BASIL AND RICOTTA SAUCE

Serves 4

Preparation time: 5 minutes + 5 minutes cooking

350 ml (12 fl oz) milk

500 g (1 lb) ricotta cheese, cut or broken into small pieces

a bunch of fresh basil, shredded

salt and pepper

Basil is a delicate, highly scented herb which should never be chopped with a knife or it will lose its pungency. Try to tear the leaves gently with your fingers or cut them carefully with a pair of kitchen scissors instead. This sauce looks very pretty with tagliatelle verdi.

In a saucepan heat the milk and ricotta over a low heat, stirring, until the ricotta melts. Remove the pan from the heat and stir in the basil. Adjust the seasoning. Serve with freshly cooked pasta.

PASTA PRIMAVERA

Preparation time: 10 minutes + 20–25 minutes cooking

250 g (8 oz) spaghetti

125 g (4 oz) green beans, topped and tailed, cut into 1 cm (½-inch) lengths

1 large carrot, cut into long, thin strips

1 large courgette, cut into long, thin strips

125 g (4 oz) shelled fresh peas, or frozen petits pois, thawed

25 g (1 oz) butter

2–3 tablespoons olive oil

2 shallots, sliced thinly

1 garlic clove, chopped

1 tablespoon chopped fresh parsley, preferably flat-leaf

1 small celery stick, sliced finely

2 tablespoons vegetable stock

salt and pepper

freshly grated parmesan cheese, to serve

Bring a large pan of salted water to the boil. Plunge the spaghetti, beans and carrot into the boiling water and cook for 5 minutes. Add the courgette and cook for 2 minutes. Add the peas and cook for 1 minute longer. Drain well.

Heat the butter and 2 tablespoons of the olive oil in a large frying pan. Add the shallots, garlic, parsley and celery and fry for 5 minutes, stirring frequently.

Add the stock and cooked pasta and vegetables to the frying pan. Mix well and heat through for 3 minutes. Taste and adjust the seasoning. If the pasta seems dry, stir in the remaining oil. Sprinkle with grated parmesan cheese and serve.

Borlotti Bean Sauce
Pasta Primavera

BORLOTTI BEAN SAUCE

Preparation time: 10 minutes + 10–15 minutes cooking

5 tablespoons olive oil

1 green pepper, de-seeded and chopped

1 small red onion, sliced thinly

1 red chilli, de-seeded and sliced

1 garlic clove, crushed

432 g (15 oz) can of borlotti beans, drained and rinsed

397 g (14 oz) can of chopped tomatoes

1 tablespoon shredded fresh basil

1 tablespoon shredded fresh parsley, preferably flat-leaf

To garnish and serve:

freshly grated parmesan cheese

fresh basil leaves

fresh parsley sprigs

I always keep some cans of borlotti beans in my cupboard for those occasions when I don't have time to shop. That way I can make this delicious sauce quickly for supper. I like to serve it with wholewheat spirals.

Heat the oil in a saucepan. Gently fry the pepper, onion, chilli and garlic for 5 minutes, stirring frequently.

Stir in the borlotti beans and tomatoes and cook for 5–10 minutes, until thickened. Stir in the herbs.

Toss the sauce with freshly cooked pasta and sprinkle with parmesan cheese. Garnish with fresh basil and parsley.

ASPARAGUS AND GINGER CREAM SAUCE

Serves 4

Preparation time: 15 minutes + 15 minutes cooking

3 tablespoons olive oil

4 shallots, chopped finely

2.5 cm (1-inch) piece of fresh root ginger, grated

750 g (1½ lb) asparagus, cut into 1 cm (½-inch) lengths

250 g (8 oz) ricotta cheese

250 g (8 oz) greek-style yogurt

salt and pepper

75 g (3 oz) parmesan cheese, grated, to serve

The Italians adore asparagus, and so do I! It is a vegetable which always reminds me that spring has arrived. The combination of asparagus and parmesan cheese is quite a popular one in Italy. I have included fresh ginger, which enhances the delicate flavour of the asparagus. Try serving it with fettuccine.

Heat the olive oil in a frying pan over a low heat and fry the shallots, ginger and asparagus for 10 minutes, stirring frequently.

In a blender or food processor combine the ricotta and yogurt until well blended. Stir into the asparagus mixture and heat for 1–2 minutes, mixing well to combine. Check the seasoning.

Toss with freshly cooked pasta and sprinkle with the grated parmesan cheese.

MINTED PEA AND CREAM SAUCE

Serves 4

Preparation time: 5 minutes + 10 minutes cooking

175 ml (6 fl oz) crème fraîche or double cream

1 small bunch of mint, shredded

275 g (9 oz) shelled peas, thawed if frozen

75 g (3 oz) butter

140 g (4½ oz) parmesan cheese, grated finely

salt and pepper

This is a lovely sauce to serve with paglia e fieno in spring, when peas and fresh mint are at their very best.

Heat the crème fraîche or double cream in a small saucepan without boiling. Remove the pan from the heat and stir in the mint. Leave to infuse for several minutes.

Cook the peas with half the butter in enough boiling water to just cover. Season well.

Combine the peas and their liquid, the cream, the remaining butter and the parmesan and reheat gently. Adjust the seasoning. Serve with freshly cooked pasta.

GINGER TOMATO SAUCE

Serves 4

Preparation time: 5 minutes + 30 minutes cooking

40 g (1½ oz) unsalted butter

175 g (6 oz) onions, chopped

2.5 cm (1-inch) piece of fresh root ginger, grated

2 garlic cloves, crushed

2 × 397 g (14 oz) can of chopped tomatoes

salt and pepper

fresh coriander leaves, to garnish

This sauce always seems to go down well with my friends, who all like ginger. Serve it with tortelloni or ravioli.

Melt the butter in a saucepan and fry the onions for about 5 minutes, stirring occasionally, until softened. Add the ginger and garlic and cook, stirring, for 2 minutes. Add the tomatoes and bring to the boil. Simmer, stirring occasionally, for 20 minutes.

Purée the mixture in a blender or food processor. Taste and adjust the seasoning. Strain the sauce through a sieve into a pan and reheat. Serve with freshly cooked pasta and garnish with fresh coriander leaves.

MEXICAN TOMATO SAUCE

Serves 4

Preparation time: 20 minutes + 40–45 minutes cooking

4 tablespoons olive oil

1 onion, chopped finely

1 garlic clove, chopped

6 extra large or 18–20 small tomatoes, skinned, de-seeded and chopped

125 ml (4 fl oz) vegetable stock

3 red chillies, de-seeded and chopped

1 teaspoon finely chopped fresh oregano

salt and pepper

fresh oregano sprigs, to garnish

Reserve this recipe for the summer, when tomatoes are at their ripest and juiciest best. Serve it with fettuccine or tagliatelle.

Heat the oil in a saucepan and fry the onion and garlic for 5 minutes. Add the tomatoes and stock and boil, uncovered, for 30–35 minutes, until thickened.

Add the chillies, oregano and seasoning and simmer for 5 minutes. Serve with freshly cooked pasta and garnish with fresh oregano.

SPINACH AND ALMOND SAUCE

Serves 4

Preparation time: 15 minutes + 10 minutes cooking

500 g (1 lb) fresh spinach

50 g (2 oz) butter

2 garlic cloves, chopped

1 tablespoon shredded fresh basil

1 bunch of parsley, preferably flat-leaf, chopped

40 g (1½ oz) parmesan cheese, grated finely

75 g (3 oz) ground almonds

3 tablespoons extra-virgin olive oil

4 tablespoons hot water

freshly grated parmesan cheese, to serve (optional)

Try this simple sauce with tagliatelle verdi.

Rinse the spinach well and transfer it to a large saucepan. Cover and cook over a gentle heat for about 5 minutes until softened. Drain well in a colander, squeezing out the excess liquid with a fork.

Melt the butter in a small saucepan and gently fry the garlic for about 3 minutes until softened. Transfer the butter and garlic to a food processor or blender and add the spinach, basil, parsley, parmesan, ground almonds, oil and water. Process until well blended. Return the mixture to the saucepan and heat gently. Serve with freshly cooked pasta and grated parmesan cheese, if wished.

MANGE TOUT, LEMON AND BASIL SAUCE

Serves 4

Preparation and cooking time: 10 minutes

250 g (8 oz) mange tout

finely grated zest and juice of 2 lemons

50 g (2 oz) butter, softened

3 tablespoons olive oil

15 g (½ oz) fresh basil leaves, shredded

4 teaspoons chopped fresh parsley, preferably flat-leaf

fresh basil leaves, to garnish

This delicate sauce makes a superb dinner party starter when served with capellini. Save a few whole basil leaves for a pretty garnish.

Steam the mange tout for 3–4 minutes over a saucepan of boiling water.

Combine the mange tout with the remaining ingredients. Serve tossed with freshly cooked pasta and garnished with fresh basil.

COLD TOMATO SAUCE WITH FETA AND ROCKET

Serves 4

Preparation time: 15 minutes + 4 hours standing

500 g (1 lb) very ripe tomatoes, skinned and chopped

6 tablespoons extra-virgin olive oil

15 g (½ oz) rocket leaves, shredded

250 g (8 oz) feta cheese, crumbled

10 black olives, pitted and sliced

pepper

This makes a lovely sauce in summer. It is particularly good with capellini.

In a large bowl mix together the tomatoes, olive oil and rocket. Season lightly with pepper. Leave the bowl, covered, at room temperature for at least 4 hours.

Before serving, stir in the feta and olives. Season with freshly ground black pepper only, as the feta and olives are quite salty. Serve mixed into hot pasta.

Variations: Substitute basil for the rocket leaves and omit the olives. Or substitute mozzarella cheese for the feta.

LEEK AND COURGETTE SAUCE

Serves 4

Preparation time: 10 minutes + 20 minutes cooking

50 g (2 oz) butter

250 g (8 oz) leeks, sliced

3 tablespoons dry white vermouth

3 tablespoons dry white wine

250 g (8 oz) courgettes, cut into small cubes

142 ml (¼ pint) carton of single cream

65 g (2½ oz) parmesan cheese, grated finely

salt and pepper

If you are lucky enough to find yellow courgettes – sometimes known by their Italian name, zucchini *– use them instead of the green variety. Equal quantities of yellow and green courgettes also make an attractive and delicious combination. Try this sauce with paglia e fieno.*

Melt the butter in a frying pan and gently fry the leeks for 5 minutes, stirring frequently. Add the vermouth and wine to the pan and continue cooking until most of the liquid has evaporated.

Add the courgettes to the pan and cook for 2 minutes, stirring. Stir in the cream and season well. Cook for 5 minutes, stirring constantly. Remove from the heat and stir in the parmesan cheese. Serve with freshly cooked pasta.

CHEESE AND HERB SAUCE

Serves 4

Preparation time: 15 minutes + 10 minutes cooking

3 eggs, beaten

3 tablespoons milk

¼ teaspoon ground nutmeg

40 g (1½ oz) butter

1 tablespoon shredded fresh parsley, preferably flat-leaf

1 tablespoon shredded fresh basil

25 g (1 oz) Gruyère cheese, grated

50 g (2 oz) parmesan cheese, grated

salt and pepper

fresh basil leaves, to garnish

This is best served with a long pasta; it goes particularly well with garlic and herb tagliatelle.

In a small saucepan, gently heat the eggs, milk and nutmeg until just warmed. Cook over a low heat for 3 minutes, stirring.

Toss freshly cooked pasta with the butter and then with the egg mixture. Add the herbs and cheeses and mix well to combine. Taste and adjust the seasoning. Garnish with fresh basil leaves and serve.

ASPARAGUS AND MUSHROOM SAUCE

Serves 4–6

Preparation time: 10 minutes + 15 minutes cooking

500 g (1 lb) asparagus, trimmed and cut diagonally into 2.5 cm (1-inch) pieces

65 g (2½ oz) butter

2 shallots, chopped finely

250 g (8 oz) shiitake mushrooms, cut in half unless small

200 ml (7 fl oz) crème fraîche or double cream

4 tablespoons chopped fresh parsley, preferably flat-leaf

2 tablespoons freshly grated parmesan cheese

salt and pepper

Oyster mushrooms make a good alternative to shiitake mushrooms in this sauce, which is great with tagliatelle or fettuccine.

Steam the asparagus for about 5 minutes until just tender.

In a large frying pan melt the butter and gently fry the shallots for 3 minutes. Add the mushrooms and cook for 5 minutes, until softened. Stir in the crème fraîche or double cream and bring to the boil. Remove from the heat and stir in the asparagus, parsley and parmesan cheese and season to taste.

Toss the sauce with freshly cooked pasta to serve.

TOMATO AND ALMOND SAUCE

Serves 4

Preparation time: 5 minutes + 15 minutes cooking

25 g (1 oz) flaked almonds

50 g (2 oz) ground almonds

3 garlic cloves, crushed with 1 teaspoon salt

25 g (1 oz) fresh basil leaves

4 tablespoons olive oil

375 g (12 oz) tomatoes, skinned, de-seeded and chopped

salt and pepper

The combination of almonds and tomatoes is often found in southern Italian cookery. It is a popular Arab combination, however, and the Arabs are credited with introducing it to the Italians. This sauce is ideal with spaghetti.

Preheat the oven to Gas Mark 4/180°C/350°F or preheat the grill. Spread the flaked almonds on a baking sheet and toast for 4 minutes. Leave to cool.

In a blender or food processor combine the ground almonds, garlic paste, basil, olive oil and tomatoes to make a smooth paste. Taste and adjust the seasoning.

In a large bowl toss the sauce with freshly

cooked pasta, thinning the mixture if necessary with hot water. Sprinkle over the toasted flaked almonds.

INDONESIAN CUCUMBER AND SPICY PEANUT SAUCE

Serves 4

Preparation time: 10 minutes

125 g (4 oz) smooth peanut butter

2 tablespoons soy sauce

juice of 1 lemon

2 garlic cloves, chopped

1/4 teaspoon dried crushed chillies

1/2 teaspoon sugar

4 tablespoons hot water

1 cucumber, peeled, halved, de-seeded and cut diagonally into 3 mm (1/8-inch) slices

1 bunch of spring onions, cut diagonally into 3 mm (1/8-inch) slices

This is a popular sauce in America, probably because peanut butter is a storecupboard staple. Do not be tempted to substitute crunchy peanut butter for the smooth variety, as you will not obtain the same result. Try this with capellini.

In a blender or food processor combine the peanut butter, soy sauce, lemon juice, garlic, chillies, sugar and water and process until smooth, adding more hot water, tablespoon by tablespoon, if the sauce seems too thick.

Transfer the sauce to a mixing bowl and combine with the cucumber and spring onions. Serve with freshly cooked pasta.

ORANGE PUMPKIN SAUCE

Serves 4

Preparation time: 15 minutes + 25 minutes cooking

25 g (1 oz) butter

2 tablespoons olive oil

2 garlic cloves, chopped finely

1 leek, cut into small strips

500 g (1 lb) pumpkin, peeled, de-seeded and cut into small cubes

150 ml (¼ pint) freshly squeezed orange juice

150 ml (¼ pint) vegetable stock

4 tablespoons single cream

finely grated zest of 1 orange

a pinch of nutmeg

salt and pepper

This is a great sauce to make in the autumn, when young pumpkins are abundant. The Italians often use pumpkin to make a lovely fresh, orange-coloured pasta, known as gnocchi. This colourful sauce looks wonderful with tagliatelle verdi.

Melt the butter and oil in a saucepan and cook the garlic and leeks for about 5 minutes or until softened, stirring.

Add the pumpkin, orange juice and stock and bring to the boil. Reduce the heat to a simmer, cover and cook for 15–20 minutes, until the pumpkin is tender when pierced with a fork.

Remove the pan from the heat and stir in the cream, orange zest and nutmeg. Reheat briefly. Adjust the seasoning. Serve with freshly cooked pasta.

BROCCOLI AND CAULIFLOWER SAUCE

Serves 4

Preparation time: 10 minutes + 30 minutes cooking

3 tablespoons olive oil

about 250 g (8 oz) cauliflower, divided into florets and stems sliced thinly

about 250 g (8 oz) broccoli, divided into florets and stems sliced thinly

2 garlic cloves, chopped

1 chilli, de-seeded and chopped

Try this sauce with paglia e fieno.

Heat the olive oil in a saucepan and fry the cauliflower, broccoli, garlic and chilli for 15 minutes over a medium heat, stirring frequently.

Add the stock and bring the mixture to the boil. Cook until reduced by half. Stir in the tomatoes and simmer for 5 minutes.

Stir the double cream into the sauce and heat through without boiling. Taste and adjust the

250 ml (8 fl oz) vegetable
stock

397 g (14 oz) can of
chopped tomatoes, drained

200 ml (7 fl oz) double
cream

salt and pepper

seasoning. Serve the sauce with freshly cooked
pasta.

SPINACH AND CHICK-PEA SAUCE

Serves 4

Preparation time: 10 minutes + 15 minutes cooking

1 large carrot, cut into long,
thin strips

25 g (1 oz) butter

2 shallots, chopped finely

1 leek, cut into long, thin
strips

125 ml (4 fl oz) dry white
wine

125 ml (4 fl oz) chicken
stock

142 ml (¼ pint) carton of
double cream

500 g (1 lb) frozen leaf
spinach, thawed

432 g (15 oz) can of chick-
peas, drained and rinsed

salt and pepper

50 g (2 oz) parmesan
cheese, grated, to serve

This sauce goes well with farfalle.

Blanch the carrot in boiling salted water for 2
minutes. Drain and rinse in cold water.

In a heavy-based saucepan melt the butter
and cook the shallots and leek for about 5
minutes until softened. Add the wine and boil
the mixture until reduced by half. Add the
stock and cream and boil for 2–3 minutes until
reduced by half again.

Squeeze as much water as possible out of the
spinach with your hands. Stir the spinach into
the sauce, together with the carrots and chick-
peas. Cook for 4–5 minutes. Taste and adjust
the seasoning.

Toss the sauce with freshly cooked pasta and
serve with the parmesan cheese.

CREAMY ARTICHOKE SAUCE

Serves 4–6

Preparation time: 10 minutes + 10 minutes cooking

Creamy Artichoke Sauce

285 g (9½ oz) jar of
Antipasti Carciofini (sliced
artichoke hearts in seasoned
oil)

25 g (1 oz) butter

1 small onion, sliced

142 ml (¼ pint) carton of
soured cream

150 g (5 oz) cottage cheese

1 tablespoon shredded fresh
basil

1 tablespoon chopped fresh
chives

a pinch of Cayenne pepper

salt and pepper

To garnish:

fresh chives

Sun-dried Tomato and
Goat's Cheese Sauce

Vegetarian Chilli Sauce

*My Father, who loves to cook and is very good at it,
gave me this recipe. I was immediately captivated as
I adore artichokes, and they combine beautifully with
soured cream, another favourite ingredient. This is
perfect served with garlic and herb tagliatelle.*

Drain the oil from the artichokes and reserve.
Roughly chop the artichokes.
   Heat the reserved artichoke liquid and the
butter in a frying pan. Add the onions and cook
for about 5 minutes until softened. Add the
chopped artichokes and heat through for about
3 minutes. Reduce the heat and stir in the
remaining ingredients, mixing well. Remove
the pan from the heat.
   Toss the sauce with freshly cooked pasta and
garnish with chives.

SUN-DRIED TOMATO AND GOAT'S CHEESE SAUCE

Serves 4

Preparation time: 10 minutes + 40 minutes cooking

25 g (1 oz) butter

2 tablespoons olive oil

1 garlic clove, chopped finely

1 onion, chopped finely

2 large carrots, chopped finely

2 celery sticks, chopped finely

397 g (14 oz) can of chopped tomatoes

125 g (4 oz) Pomodori Secchi (sun-dried tomatoes in seasoned oil), drained and chopped roughly

125 ml (4 fl oz) white wine

125 g (4 oz) soft goat's cheese, crumbled

8 Calamata olives

salt and pepper

fresh parsley sprigs, preferably flat-leaf, to garnish

Although the ingredients for this sauce are currently popular, both sun-dried tomatoes and goat's cheese have been around for centuries! Serve it with farfalle.

Heat the butter and oil in a saucepan. Add the garlic, onion, carrot and celery and fry for 10 minutes, until slightly softened, stirring frequently.

Stir in the tomatoes, sun-dried tomatoes and wine. Season to taste. Simmer, covered, for about 30 minutes, stirring occasionally.

Toss the sauce, goat's cheese and olives with freshly cooked pasta. Garnish with fresh parsley sprigs.

VEGETARIAN CHILLI SAUCE

Serves 4

Preparation time: 25 minutes + 40 minutes cooking

2 tablespoons oil

2.5 cm (1-inch) piece of
fresh root ginger, peeled
and grated finely

1 onion, chopped

1 garlic clove, chopped

1 green pepper, de-seeded
and chopped

1/2 teaspoon cumin

2 celery sticks, chopped

2 carrots, chopped

1 courgette, chopped

397 g (14 oz) can of
chopped tomatoes

150 ml (1/4 pint) vegetable
stock

1/4 teaspoon chilli powder

1/2 teaspoon dried oregano

432 g (15 oz) can of red
kidney beans, drained

439 g (15 oz) can of butter
beans, drained

*This sauce is exceptionally easy to make and the
ginger gives it a special flavour. I like to serve it on
tortelloni or fusilli tricolori.*

Heat the oil in a pan and fry the ginger, onion,
garlic and green pepper for 5 minutes. Add all
the remaining ingredients, except the beans,
and simmer over a low heat, covered, for 30
minutes.
   Add the beans and simmer for a further
5 minutes. Serve with freshly cooked pasta.

BROCCOLI AND WALNUT SAUCE

Serves 4

Preparation time: 5 minutes + 10 minutes cooking

Tomato and Basil Cream Sauce

500 g (1 lb) broccoli	*Try this sauce with farfalle.*
25 g (1 oz) butter	Trim the broccoli. Separate the heads into florets and thinly slice the stalks.
1 small onion, chopped	Melt the butter in a heavy-based saucepan and gently fry the onion for 5 minutes. Add the broccoli and cook for 5 minutes. Stir in the cheese and milk and stir until the cheese melts and the sauce thickens. Taste and adjust the seasoning.
150 g (5 oz) full-fat soft cheese with garlic and herbs, cubed	
300 ml (½ pint) milk	
75 g (3 oz) walnut pieces	Remove the pan from the heat and toss the sauce with freshly cooked pasta and the walnuts. Serve with grated parmesan.
salt and pepper	
freshly grated parmesan cheese, to serve	

Broccoli and Walnut Sauce

Rocket, Pine Kernel and Parmesan Sauce

TOMATO AND BASIL CREAM SAUCE

Serves 4–6

Preparation time: 20 minutes + about 5 minutes cooking

284 ml (½ pint) carton of
double cream

300 ml (½ pint) vegetable
stock

125 ml (4 fl oz) water

150 ml (¼ pint) olive oil

300 g (10 oz) tomatoes,
skinned, de-seeded and
cubed

a large bunch of fresh basil
leaves (about 50 g/2 oz),
shredded

3 tablespoons freshly grated
parmesan cheese

fresh basil leaves, to
garnish

*Serve this sauce with a long pasta such as fettuccine
or tagliatelle.*

In a saucepan combine the cream, stock, water
and oil. Bring to a boil and cook the mixture
vigorously for 5 minutes. Add the tomatoes
and basil and simmer for 1 minute.

Toss the sauce with freshly cooked pasta and
the parmesan. Serve garnished with fresh basil
leaves.

ROCKET, PINE KERNEL AND PARMESAN SAUCE

Serves 4

Preparation time: 5 minutes + 5–10 minutes cooking

75 g (3 oz) pine kernels

6 tablespoons olive oil

75 g (3 oz) rocket leaves

75 g (3 oz) parmesan
cheese, grated finely

salt and pepper

Rocket (Roquette), also known as arugula, *a
peppery leaf traditionally used in salads, makes a
terrific pairing with pasta. Try it with capellini.*

Preheat the oven to Gas Mark 4/180°C/350°F or
preheat the grill. Spread the pine kernels on a
baking sheet and toast for 5 minutes, then cool.

Heat the oil in a frying pan. Add the rocket
and fry, stirring, for 30 seconds.

Stir the rocket into freshly cooked pasta
which has been drained and returned to its pan.
Stir in the parmesan. Taste and adjust the
seasoning. Transfer to a large serving bowl and
sprinkle with the toasted pine kernels.

SPAGHETTI VERDI FRITTATA

Preparation time: 5 minutes + 15–25 minutes cooking

125 g (4 oz) dried spaghetti verdi, or 250 g (8 oz) cooked leftover spaghetti verdi

3 tablespoons olive oil

25 g (1 oz) parmesan cheese, grated

25 g (1 oz) mozzarella cheese, grated

1 large garlic clove, chopped finely

salt and pepper

¼ quantity of Mexican Tomato Sauce (page 64) heated, to serve

This is a great way to use up leftover spaghetti, but you can also enjoy it with freshly cooked spaghetti. Serve with a watercress salad.

If using dried spaghetti, cook it in plenty of boiling salted water according to the packet instructions. Drain.

Toss the spaghetti with 2 teaspoons of the olive oil. Mix in the cheeses and garlic. Taste and adjust the seasoning.

Heat 2 tablespoons of the remaining oil in a non-stick 25 cm (10-inch) frying pan. Add the pasta mixture and gently press down with a spatula to spread out evenly. Cook for 6–8 minutes, pressing down occasionally, until golden brown on one side.

Gently loosen the frittata from the pan and invert it onto a plate. Slide back into the pan, adding a little more of the oil if necessary. Cook for 6–8 minutes longer.

Serve the frittata with the Mexican Tomato Sauce.

TRE COLORE SAUCE

Preparation time: 15 minutes + 1–4 hours standing

750 g (1½ lb) ripe tomatoes, de-seeded and chopped

3 garlic cloves, chopped finely

a large bunch of fresh basil, shredded

125 g (4 oz) mozzarella cheese, cubed

125 ml (4 fl oz) extra-virgin olive oil

2 tablespoons balsamic vinegar

salt and pepper

This no-cook sauce is one of my family's favourites in summer. Tre colore means 'three colours' and refers to the colours of the Italian flag, which is red, white and green. Try it with capellini.

Combine all the ingredients in a large bowl, mixing well. Season with salt and pepper. Leave to stand at room temperature, covered, for at least 1 hour, or up to 4 hours. Serve mixed into hot pasta.

BAKED PASTA DISHES

PROSCIUTTO, RICOTTA AND BASIL LASAGNE

Preparation time: 35 minutes + 20 minutes cooking

50 g (2 oz) butter

50 g (2 oz) plain flour

a pinch of nutmeg

450 ml (¾ pint) milk

125 g (4 oz) prosciutto crudo, cut into strips

1 large bunch of fresh basil, shredded

125 g (4 oz) ricotta cheese, crumbled

50 g (2 oz) parmesan cheese, grated finely

175 g (6 oz) no pre-cook lasagne verdi, boiled for 10 minutes

salt and pepper

fresh basil leaves, to garnish

This is a much lighter and more delicate version of traditional Baked Lasagne (page 83), made with a white sauce instead of the meat sauce. It is perfect for a light lunch or supper dish. You will need to boil the lasagne before using it because of the short baking time.

Preheat the oven to Gas Mark 6/200°C/400°F. Grease a 28 × 23 cm (11- × 9-inch) ovenproof dish.

Melt the butter in a small saucepan and stir in the flour, nutmeg and salt and pepper. Cook for 1 minute, stirring constantly. Stir in the milk a little at a time and whisk for about 2 minutes until thickened. Remove from the heat and stir in the prosciutto, basil, ricotta and half the parmesan. Taste and adjust the seasoning.

Place a layer of the lasagne in the ovenproof dish. Top with a layer of the ricotta mixture and sprinkle with some of the remaining parmesan cheese. Repeat the layers, finishing with the last of the sauce and parmesan.

Bake the lasagne in the oven for 20 minutes. Garnish with fresh basil leaves and serve.

MACARONI AND CHEESE

Serves 4

Preparation time: 15 minutes + 30–35 minutes cooking

250 g (8 oz) macaroni

50 g (2 oz) butter

50 g (2 oz) plain flour

600 ml (1 pint) milk

175 g (6 oz) Gorgonzola
cheese, chopped

65 g (2½ oz) parmesan
cheese, grated finely

65 g (2½ oz) wholemeal
breadcrumbs, toasted

salt and pepper

*This is my husband's favourite pasta dish. I think he
would eat it seven days a week without growing tired
of it. Toast the breadcrumbs on a baking sheet in
the oven while preparing the dish – they take about
10 minutes.*

Preheat the oven to Gas Mark 4/180°C/350°F.
Cook the macaroni in plenty of boiling salted
water, according to the packet instructions.
Drain well.

Melt the butter in a saucepan, stir in the flour
and cook for 1–2 minutes, stirring
continuously. Remove the pan from the heat
and gradually stir in the milk. Return the pan to
the heat and cook, stirring, until the sauce is
thickened. Remove the pan from the heat and
stir in the cooked pasta and the cheeses. Season
with salt and pepper.

Spoon the mixture into a 1.2-litre (2-pint)
shallow, ovenproof dish and sprinkle over the
breadcrumbs. Bake in the oven for 30–35
minutes.

Variations: For a milder version, substitute
equal quantities of grated Cheddar and Gruyère
cheese for the Gorgonzola. Or try using a
different pasta shape, such as penne or fusilli.

BAKED LASAGNE

Preparation time: 30 minutes + 1 hour cooking + 5 minutes standing

1–2 garlic cloves, chopped finely

1 onion, chopped

2 tablespoons olive oil

500 g (1 lb) minced beef

2 quantities of Mushroom and Tomato Sauce (page 27) or Mexican Tomato Sauce (page 64), or a 350 g (11 oz) jar of Classic Italian Sauce with Mushrooms

75 g (3 oz) tomato purée

175 ml (6 fl oz) water

1/2 teaspoon dried oregano

1/4 teaspoon dried basil

50 g (2 oz) provolone cheese, grated

250 g (8 oz) no pre-cook lasagne verdi

250 g (8 oz) ricotta cheese, crumbled

125 g (4 oz) mozzarella cheese, grated

25 g (1 oz) parmesan cheese, grated

salt and pepper

This recipe doubles easily and is perfect for entertaining large crowds as part of a buffet. If you can't find provolone cheese, use extra mozzarella instead.

Preheat the oven to Gas Mark 4/180°C/350°F. Grease a 28 × 23 cm (11- × 9-inch) ovenproof dish.

In a large saucepan fry the garlic and onion in the oil for 5 minutes. Add the meat and cook for 5 minutes until brown all over. Add the sauce, tomato purée, water, oregano and basil. Cover and simmer for 10 minutes. Taste and adjust the seasoning.

Pour a third of the meat sauce into the ovenproof dish. Sprinkle with half the provolone and then cover with a layer of lasagne. Spread half the ricotta and mozarella cheese over the lasagne. Repeat the layers, ending with meat sauce. Sprinkle with parmesan cheese and cover with foil.

Bake the lasagne in the oven for 50 minutes. Remove the foil and continue baking for a further 10 minutes. Leave to stand for 5 minutes before serving.

MIDDLE EASTERN LAMB AND COURGETTE GRATIN

Serves 4

Preparation time: 5 minutes + about 40 minutes cooking

1 onion, sliced

1–2 garlic cloves, chopped finely

3 tablespoons olive oil

¼ teaspoon ground cinnamon

¼ teaspoon allspice

300 g (10 oz) minced lamb

397 g (14 oz) can of chopped tomatoes

300 g (10 oz) courgettes, sliced

175 g (6 oz) conchiglie

50 g (2 oz) parmesan cheese, grated

salt and pepper

Middle Eastern Lamb and Courgette Gratin

Baked Lasagne

Preheat the oven to Gas Mark 6/200°C/400°F.

Fry the onion and garlic in the oil for 5 minutes. Add the spices and cook for 1 minute. Add the lamb and cook for 5 minutes. Add the tomatoes and courgettes and season. Simmer for 10 minutes.

Cook the pasta in boiling salted water, according to the packet instructions. Drain.

Mix the pasta with the meat mixture and transfer to a 1.2-litre (2-pint) greased ovenproof dish. Sprinkle with the grated parmesan. Bake in the oven for 10 minutes. Brown under a hot grill for 2–3 minutes before serving.

Spinach and Mushroom Cannelloni with Cheese Sauce

SPINACH AND MUSHROOM CANNELLONI WITH CHEESE SAUCE

Serves 4

Preparation time: 40 minutes + 25–30 minutes cooking

125 g (4 oz) (about 12) dried cannelloni tubes

For the filling:

75 g (3 oz) butter

1 onion, chopped finely

125 g (4 oz) chestnut mushrooms, sliced thinly

500 g (1 lb) frozen spinach, thawed and chopped

50 g (2 oz) parmesan cheese, grated finely

salt and pepper

For the sauce:

50 g (2 oz) butter

4 tablespoons plain flour

600 ml (1 pint) milk

75 g (3 oz) mozzarella cheese, grated

75 g (3 oz) Gruyère cheese, grated

salt and pepper

Preheat the oven to Gas Mark 6/200°C/400°F. Grease a 28 × 23 cm (11- × 9-inch) ovenproof dish.

To make the cannelloni filling, melt the butter in a saucepan, add the onion and fry for 5 minutes. Add the mushrooms and cook for 3–5 minutes. Squeeze as much water as possible out of the spinach with your hands. Add the spinach and boil for about 5 minutes until most of the water has evaporated. Remove from the heat. Stir in the parmesan. Taste and adjust the seasoning.

To make the sauce, melt the butter in a saucepan. Stir in the flour and cook for 1 minute, stirring. Remove the pan from the heat and gradually stir in the milk. Bring slowly to the boil and continue to cook, stirring continuously, until the sauce has thickened. Remove the pan from the heat and stir in three-quarters of the cheeses, stirring until melted. Taste and adjust the seasoning.

Pour enough of the sauce into the ovenproof dish to just cover the bottom. Spoon the spinach filling into the cannelloni tubes and arrange them side by side in the dish. Pour over the remaining sauce.

Sprinkle with the remaining cheese and bake in the oven for 25–30 minutes.

PASTA SHELLS FLORENTINE

Serves 4–6

Preparation time: 25 minutes + 30–40 minutes cooking

500 g (1 lb) frozen
spinach, thawed and
chopped

300 g (10 oz) ricotta
cheese, crumbled

75 g (3 oz) parmesan
cheese, grated

1 tablespoon chopped fresh
basil

2 garlic cloves, crushed

250 g (8 oz) Venetian
pasta shells

2 quantities of Baked
Tomato Sauce (page 15)

salt and pepper

To garnish and serve:

fresh basil leaves

freshly grated parmesan
cheese

*This attractive dish makes a great starter for a dinner
party. Or serve it as a light supper dish with a crisp
green salad and hot garlic bread.*

Preheat the oven to Gas Mark 4/180°C/350°F.

Squeeze as much water out of the spinach as
possible with your hands. In a bowl mix the
spinach with the ricotta, half the parmesan, the
basil and garlic. Taste and adjust the seasoning.

Cook the pasta shells in plenty of boiling
salted water, according to the packet
instructions. Drain well.

Spoon 125 ml (4 fl oz) of the Baked Tomato
Sauce over the bottom of a 28 × 23 cm (11- ×
9-inch) ovenproof dish. Fill each shell with
some of the spinach mixture. Place the filled
shells in the dish and spoon the remaining sauce
over the shells. Sprinkle with the remaining
parmesan cheese.

Cover the dish loosely with foil and bake in
the oven for 30–40 minutes until heated
through. Garnish with fresh basil leaves and
serve with parmesan cheese.

PASTA EN PAPILLOTE

Serves 4

Preparation time: 15 minutes + 35 minutes cooking

2 tablespoons olive oil

1 garlic clove, chopped

397 g (14 oz) can of chopped tomatoes

¼ teaspoon dried crushed chillies

175 g (6 oz) quick-cook spaghetti

125 g (4 oz) mozzarella cheese, cubed

12 black olives, pitted and quartered

4 tablespoons shredded fresh basil

salt and pepper

fresh basil leaves, to garnish

A great dinner party starter, it looks terrific and stays hot until each 'packet' is opened.

Preheat the oven to Gas Mark 5/190°C/375°F. Brush four 30 × 30 cm (12- × 12-inch) pieces of baking parchment with oil and place on lightly oiled baking sheets.

Heat the oil in a saucepan and fry the garlic for 2 minutes. Add the tomatoes and crushed chillies and season with salt and pepper. Cook for 15–20 minutes, uncovered, stirring occasionally.

Cook the pasta for 3 minutes in boiling salted water. Drain and then mix with the tomato sauce, mozzarella, olives and basil.

Divide the pasta mixture equally between the pieces of baking parchment (1). Wrap the parchment tightly, twisting each end to seal firmly (2). Bake in the oven for 15 minutes. Serve garnished with fresh basil.

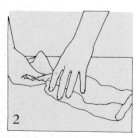

Spaghetti Pie
Pasta en Papillote

SPAGHETTI PIE

Preparation time: 30 minutes + 20–30 minutes cooking

For the crust:

175 g (6 oz) vermicelli,
broken into 2.5 cm (1-inch)
lengths, cooked and drained

1 garlic clove, chopped
finely

50 g (2 oz) butter

50 g (2 oz) parmesan
cheese, grated

1 large egg (size 1), beaten

1 tablespoon chopped fresh
basil

For the filling:

250 g (8 oz) minced beef

375 g (12 oz) chorizo
sausage, chopped

1 onion, chopped

2 quantities of Mexican
Tomato Sauce (page 64) or
a 550 g (1 lb 2 oz) jar of
Classic Italian Sauce with
Mixed Peppers

2 tablespoons tomato purée

1 teaspoon sugar

1 tablespoon chopped fresh
basil

1 tablespoon chopped fresh
oregano

50 ml (2 fl oz) dry white
wine

250 ml (8 fl oz) soured
cream

150 g (5 oz) mozzarella
cheese, grated

*Children love this dish, perhaps because its name
sounds fun! It can be served hot or at room
temperature.*

Preheat the oven to Gas Mark 4/180°C/350°F.

To make the crust, combine the vermicelli
with the remaining crust ingredients. Press into
a 25 cm (10-inch) spring-form cake tin.

To make the filling, cook the minced beef,
chorizo sausage and onion together. Drain off
the fat and then stir in the sauce, tomato purée,
sugar, herbs and wine. Heat through for 1–2
minutes.

To assemble the pie, spread the soured cream
on the crust. Top with the filling and then
sprinkle with the grated mozzarella.

Bake the pie in the oven for 20–30 minutes,
until golden brown. Cool briefly before
removing from the tin. Serve garnished with
fresh basil and oregano.

Variation: To make a vegetarian filling,
replace the minced beef and sausage with
pulses. Fry the onion in 2 tablespoons of
vegetable oil for 5 minutes until softened. Drain
a 432 g (15 oz) can of red kidney beans, a 432 g
(15 oz) can of borlotti beans and a 220 g (7 oz)
can of butter beans and stir the beans into the
onion. Add the sauce, tomato purée, sugar,
herbs and wine and heat through.

ITALIAN SPAGHETTI OMELETTE

Serves 4

Preparation time: 10 minutes + 10 minutes cooking

250 g (8 oz) leftover spaghetti and sauce, or 125 g (4 oz) dried spaghetti, cooked and tossed with ½ quantity of Pommarola (Neapolitan tomato sauce, page 12) or Mexican Tomato Sauce (page 64)

4 eggs, beaten lightly

125 g (4 oz) parmesan cheese, grated finely

2 tablespoons finely chopped fresh parsley, preferably flat-leaf

75 g (3 oz) butter

salt and pepper

To garnish and serve:

fresh parsley sprigs

1 quantity of Mushroom and Tomato Sauce (page 27), heated

toasted bread rounds

Preheat the oven to Gas Mark 6/200°C/400°F if using.

In a bowl mix together the spaghetti and sauce, eggs, cheese and parsley. Adjust the seasoning.

Melt the butter in a 20 cm (8-inch) ovenproof pan or frying pan over a medium heat. Pour in the egg mixture. With a wooden spoon move the edges of the mixture towards the centre of the pan several times until the egg mixture is set along the edge.

Transfer the pan to the oven or place under a preheated grill. Bake or grill for 5 minutes or until the omelette is set and puffy, but not browned.

Slide the omelette onto a large round plate and cut into quarters. Garnish with parsley sprigs and serve with the Mushroom and Tomato Sauce and toasted bread rounds.

STUFFED PEPPERS

Serves 4

Preparation time: 30 minutes + 45–50 minutes cooking

2 large red peppers

2 large yellow peppers

For the stuffing:

125 g (4 oz) small pasta shapes, e.g. quick-cook macaroni

1 extra large tomato, skinned and chopped

2 tablespoons olive oil, plus extra for brushing

1 small onion, chopped finely

1 garlic clove, crushed

a pinch of Cayenne pepper

2 tablespoons sultanas

2 tablespoons pine kernels

1 tablespoon finely chopped fresh parsley, preferably flat-leaf

salt and pepper

To serve:

2 quantities of Mexican Tomato Sauce (page 64), heated

A departure from the traditional rice stuffing. This is a substantial main course dish. Serve it with a robust Hungarian red wine.

Preheat the oven to Gas Mark 4/180°C/350°F. Cut the tops off the peppers and reserve. Remove the seeds.

Cook the pasta in plenty of boiling salted water, according to the packet instructions. Drain and transfer to a bowl. Add the chopped tomato and mix well.

Heat the olive oil in a small saucepan and fry the onion and garlic for about 5 minutes until softened. Stir in the Cayenne pepper, sultanas, pine kernels and parsley. Taste and adjust the seasoning. Cook for about 3 minutes until the pine kernels are lightly browned. Add to the pasta mixture, stirring well.

Divide the stuffing between the peppers and replace their tops. Brush lightly with olive oil and bake in the oven for 45–50 minutes, or until tender. Serve with the Mexican Tomato Sauce.

*Baked Penne with Dolcelatte Cheese and Radicchio
Stuffed Peppers*

BAKED PENNE WITH DOLCELATTE CHEESE AND RADICCHIO

Serves 4

Preparation time: 15 minutes + 15 minutes cooking

250 g (8 oz) penne rigate

50 g (2 oz) butter

250 g (8 oz) button mushrooms, sliced

2 garlic cloves, chopped finely

1 tablespoon finely chopped fresh sage

1 small head of radicchio (250–275 g/8–9 oz), cored and shredded finely

250 ml (8 fl oz) double cream

50 g (2 oz) parmesan cheese, grated finely

175 g (6 oz) dolcelatte cheese, cubed

salt and pepper

fresh sage leaves, to garnish

This is an unusual but delicious combination of flavours. The radicchio and penne make a striking presentation. Try using goat's cheese instead of the dolcelatte.

Preheat the oven to Gas Mark 8/230°C/450°F. Butter a 23 × 28 cm (9- × 11- inch) ovenproof dish.

Cook the pasta in boiling salted water, according to the packet instructions. Drain.

Melt the butter in a large frying pan and fry the mushrooms and garlic for about 5 minutes until softened. Stir in the sage and radicchio and remove the pan from the heat.

In a large bowl stir together the cream, parmesan and dolcelatte. Add the mushroom mixture and pasta. Taste and adjust the seasoning.

Transfer the mixture to the ovenproof dish and bake in the oven for 12–15 minutes, or until the top is browned and bubbly. Serve garnished with fresh sage leaves.

INDEX TO RECIPES

Amatrice Sauce   16
Anchovies:
  Anchovy and Rocket
    Sauce   31
  Broccoli and Anchovy
    Sauce   43
  Chicken and Anchovy
    Sauce   44
  Mushroom Sauce with
    Anchovies   30
  Puttanesca Sauce   29
  Tuna Niçoise Sauce   46
Artichokes:
  Creamy Artichoke
    Sauce   72
Asparagus and Ginger
  Cream Sauce   63
Asparagus and Mushroom
  Sauce   68
Aubergine and Cheese
  Sauce   59
Avocados:
  Guacamole Sauce   58

Bacon:
  Amatrice Sauce   16
  Bacon and Cheese
    Sauce   27
  Bacon and Rosemary
    Sauce   18
  Bacon and Spinach
    Sauce   48
  Carbonara Sauce   16
Baked Bean and Sausage
  Sauce   38
Basil and Ricotta Sauce   59
Basil Sauce   18
Beef:
  Baked Lasagne   83
  Bolognese Sauce   23
  Meatballs in Tomato
    Sauce   34
  Minced Meat and Pea
    Sauce   48
  Spaghetti Pie   90
Borlotti Bean Sauce   62
Broccoli and Anchovy
  Sauce   43
Broccoli and Cauliflower
  Sauce   70
Broccoli and Walnut
  Sauce   76

Cacciatora Sauce   26
Calamari Sauce   19
Carbonara Sauce   16
Cheese:
  Aubergine and Cheese
    Sauce   59
  Bacon and Cheese
    Sauce   27
  Baked Penne with
    Dolcelatte Cheese and
    Radicchio   94
  Basil and Ricotta
    Sauce   59
  Cheese and Herb
    Sauce   67
  Cold Tomato Sauce with
    Feta and Rocket   66
  Creamy Cheese
    Sauce   21
  Gorgonzola Sauce   26
  Macaroni and
    Cheese   82
  Prosciutto, Ricotta and
    Basil Lasagne   81
  Rocket, Pine Kernel and
    Parmesan Sauce   78
  Spinach and Mushroom
    Cannelloni with Cheese
    Sauce   86
  Spinach and Ricotta
    Sauce   14
  Sun-Dried Tomato and
    Goat's Cheese
    Sauce   74
Chicken and Anchovy
  Sauce   44
Chicken Liver and Green
  Bean Sauce   43
Chicken Sauce with
  Marsala   39
Chick-peas:
  Spinach and Chick-pea
    Sauce   71
Clams:
  Seafood Sauce   14
Cod:
  Mediterranean Cod
    Sauce   46
Coriander and Parsley
  Pesto   54
Courgette and Prosciutto
  Sauce   47

Crab and Pesto Sauce   39

Eggs:
  Italian Spaghetti
    Omelette   91

Ginger Tomato Sauce   64
Guacamole Sauce   58

Lamb:
  Lebanese Lamb and
    Spinach Sauce   42
  Middle Eastern Lamb
    and Courgette
    Gratin   84
  Minced Meat and Pea
    Sauce   48
Lasagne:
  Baked Lasagne   83
  Prosciutto, Ricotta and
    Basil Lasagne   81
Leek and Courgette
  Sauce   66

Macaroni and Cheese   82
Mange Tout, Lemon and
  Basil Sauce   65
Monkfish:
  Pink and White Seafood
    Sauce   49
Mushrooms:
  Asparagus and
    Mushroom Sauce   68
  Garlic Mushroom
    Sauce   53
  Mushroom and Pea
    Sauce   58
  Mushroom and Tomato
    Sauce   27
  Mushroom Sauce with
    Anchovies   30
  Shiitake Mushroom and
    Sage Sauce   51
  Spinach and Mushroom
    Cannelloni with Cheese
    Sauce   86
  Veal and Mushroom
    Sauce   22
Mussels:
  Mussel, Spinach and
    Leek Sauce   36
  Seafood Sauce   14

Onions:
Four–onion Sauce 55

Parsley:
Coriander and Parsley
Pesto 54
Crispy Parsley and
Breadcrumb Sauce 22
Pasta en Papillote 88
Pasta Primavera 60
Pasta Shells Florentine 87
Peanut butter:
Indonesian Cucumber
and Spicy Peanut
Sauce 69
Peas:
Minced Meat and Pea
Sauce 48
Minted Pea and Cream
Sauce 63
Mushroom and Pea
Sauce 58
Pasta Primavera 60
Veal, Wine and Pea
Sauce 24
Peppers:
Grilled Mediterranean
Vegetable Sauce 54
Peperonata 56
Roasted Red Pepper
Sauce 56
Stuffed Peppers 92
Pesto 18
Pommarola 12
Pork:
Cacciatora Sauce 26
Meatballs in Tomato
Sauce 34
Pork Paprikash
Sauce 34
Prawns:
Pink and White Seafood
Sauce 49
Prawn and Mange Tout
Sauce 32
Prosciutto:
Courgette and Prosciutto
Sauce 47
Creamy Spinach and
Prosciutto Sauce 36
Prosciutto, Ricotta and
Basil Lasagne 81
Pumpkin:
Orange Pumpkin
Sauce 70

Puttanesca Sauce 29

Radicchio:
Baked Penne with
Dolcelatte Cheese and
Radicchio 94
Ragù alla Bolognese 23
Rocket:
Anchovy and Rocket
Sauce 31
Cold Tomato Sauce with
Feta and Rocket 66
Rocket, Pine Kernel and
Parmesan Sauce 78

Salmon, smoked:
Smoked Salmon and
Asparagus Sauce 40
Smoked Salmon
Sauce 31
Salsa Piccante 29
Sardine Sauce 28
Scallop Sauce 50
Seafood Sauce 14
Spaghetti Pie 90
Spaghetti Verdi
Frittata 79
Spinach and Almond
Sauce 65
Spinach and Chick-pea
Sauce 71
Spinach and Mushroom
Cannelloni with Cheese
Sauce 86
Spinach and Ricotta
Sauce 14
Squid:
Calamari Sauce 19
Sugo di Noci 11

Tomatoes:
Baked Tomato
Sauce 15
Cold Tomato Sauce with

Feta and Rocket 66
Ginger Tomato
Sauce 64
Grilled Mediterranean
Vegetable Sauce 54
Meatballs in Tomato
Sauce 34
Mexican Tomato
Sauce 64
Mushroom and Tomato
Sauce 27
Neapolitan Tomato
Sauce 12
Piquant Sauce 29
Puttanesca Sauce 29
Sun-Dried Tomato and
Goat's Cheese
Sauce 74
Tomato and Almond
Sauce 68
Tomato and Basil Cream
Sauce 78
Tomato Sauce with
Tuna 47
Tre Colore Sauce 80
Trout, smoked:
Smoked Trout and Fish
Roe Sauce with
Chives 40
Tuna:
Tomato Sauce with
Tuna 47
Tuna Niçoise Sauce 46
Turkey:
Spicy Ground Turkey
Sauce 35

Veal and Mushroom
Sauce 22
Veal, Wine and Pea
Sauce 24
Vegetarian Chilli Sauce 7

Walnut Sauce 11

Cover design: Barry Lowenhoff
Cover illustration: Sally Swabey
Text design: Ken Vail
Photography: Patrick McLeavey
Styling: Marian Price
Food preparation for photography: Frances Cleary
Illustration: John Woodcock
Typesetting: Goodfellow & Egan, Cambridge